W9-CTF-214

HOW TO WRITE A WINNING RESUME

HOW TO WRITE A WINNING RESUME

Deborah Perlmutter Bloch

Printed on recyclable paper

 **VGM Career Horizons**
a division of *NTC Publishing Group*
Lincolnwood, Illinois USA

Acknowledgments

My thanks go to the many friends and colleagues who participated in the interviews for this book and shared many examples of résumés.

A very special thank you must be said to my husband, Martin Bloch, who provided essential support ranging from alphabetizing to zucchini slicing.

Author's note: the names of all individuals and companies, the addresses and phone numbers used in examples, sample résumés, and cover letters in this book are fictional.

Library of Congress Cataloging-in-Publication Data

Bloch, Deborah Perlmutter.
    How to write a winning resume / Deborah Perlmutter Bloch. — 3rd
ed.

    p.   cm.
    Includes bibliographical references.
    ISBN 0-8442-4172-5
    1. Résumés (Employment)   I. Title.
    HF5383.B53
    650.14—dc20   93-14223
                                                                            CIP

1995 Printing

Published by VGM Career Horizons, a division of NTC Publishing Group
4255 West Touhy Avenue
Lincolnwood (Chicago), Illinois 60646-1975, U.S.A.

5 6 7 8 9 0 VP 9 8 7 6 5 4 3

Contents

About the Author

Deborah Perlmutter Bloch, Ph.D., is an associate professor of educational administration at Baruch College, the City University of New York. Previously, she worked as the director of MetroGuide, New York City's computer-based Career Information System; the coordinator of research for the Office of Occupational and Career Education of the New York City Board of Education; a high school guidance counselor; and an English teacher.

As a consultant, Dr. Bloch has worked with the National Career Information System at the University of Oregon, New York City's Job Center and the Dropout Prevention Program, and the Departments of Labor and Education of several states. She is currently involved in the development of career counseling courses for the University of Wollongong in Australia.

Dr. Bloch is past-president of the National Career Development Association and the Association of Computer-

Based Systems for Career Information. She remains active in these groups, as well as in the guidance division of the American Vocational Association.

She has published many articles in professional and popular magazines and given numerous presentations and workshops for counselors and teachers on how to help people with their career decisions and job searches.

How to use this book: Read this before you begin!

In the tight job market of the 1990s your résumé is the essential spark that can jump start your way to economic success. Your résumé is your opportunity to present the facts of your life in a way that speaks directly to the audience you want to reach.

Who is the audience for your résumé? Are you looking for a first job, a new job, or a turnabout in career direction? The audience is each potential employer. There is also a new and growing way to work called contract employment. Contract workers provide specific services to businesses as they need them. If you want to take advantage of this end of the job market and independently contract out your services, your résumé provides the written evidence of your experience and ability to the audience—the individual in the organization responsible for choosing the service.

If you have a variety of skills and services to offer, you can successfully run a "portfolio career." This means you are offering contracted services of varied types to equally varied businesses. Each edition of your résumé can be geared to the service buyer whose needs you want to meet.

Even if you want to go into business on your own, a résumé is probably needed as part of your business plan to convince prospective investors of your expertise and experience.

You know why you want to write a résumé, but you may not be sure how to go about it. Questions of what to include and how to show yourself to best advantage are common. You may have heard terms like *functional* or *chronological* résumé and wonder what they should mean to you. This book will help you understand what to include in your résumé and how to present your information to the best advantage.

You may also have seen ads in newspapers and magazines for "experts" who can help you prepare a résumé, and at this point, you may not really be sure that you should tackle this job on your own. Eliminate any self-doubt. *You are the best person to write your résumé, because no one can know you, your skills, interests, and goals as well as you do.* A professional résumé writer might be able to make the job seem easier, but you will find that you can do just as good a job on your own. And this book will help you make it even better.

This book will provide a step-by-step guide to help you through the résumé writing process. Your questions on what to include to put your best foot forward will be answered, and you will find by the time you finish the book that you understand the process very well.

The Purpose of A Résumé

The purpose of a résumé is to get you considered for a job. It's not likely that anyone has ever gotten a job solely on the basis of her or his résumé, but people often lose the chance to be considered in the first place because of poorly written or presented résumés.

Many of the suggestions included in this book are based on the advice of actual employers in industries such as banking, computers, insurance, advertising, accounting, education, health services, law, merchandising, and others. The people surveyed are responsible for hiring employees from entry-level jobs through middle management positions and experienced professionals to the highest-level executives. Although the employers came from a variety of fields, and they themselves ranged in age from 25 to over

65, their responses to the questions were remarkably similar. Therefore, when you see a quotation from the survey, you can know that one employer said it, but the thought represents the responses of many. The step-by-step approach used in this book is designed to help you produce the kind and quality of information that these professional managers have stated specifically that they want to see.

The purpose of the résumé is to get you an interview! The résumé must catch the attention of the reader so that it goes in the pile "to be considered," rather than the pile "to be discarded." A résumé that makes the first pile and stays on top of it is a winning résumé.

Your Goals

Your goal is to produce a winning résumé—and there are essential steps in the logical sequence of right moves to reach that goal.

Step 1. Explore the details of your life for skills and accomplishments, names, dates, and places.

Step 2. Translate your skills and accomplishments into power terms and the language of the job you are seeking in the industry that interests you.

Step 3. Present the material in a way that holds the attention of the reader and reveals the very best about you.

Step 4. Write a cover letter that provides direction to the reader of your résumé—your prospective employer or buyer of your services.

The chapters of this book will help you through these steps to reach your goal—a winning résumé.

Chapter 1, "Building Blocks," includes a series of work sheets on which you will explore and develop your educational and occupational history. It includes a self-assessment questionnaire which will pinpoint the relationships between your abilities and a number of jobs.

Chapter 2, "Actions Speak Louder than Words—Use Verbs!" shows you how to translate the building blocks into active, effective statements for your résumé.

By the time you finish *Chapter 3, "Assembly,"* you will have a draft of your résumé.

In *Chapter 4, "Getting Physical,"* you will learn details of paper, layout, and typing. The mystique surrounding word processing, paper selection, and reproduction will be eliminated, probably saving you some money. *Chapter 4* concludes with specific directions for proofreading your résumé.

You will see in *Chapter 5, "Made to Order,"* how your résumé can be tailored to reach employers in different fields, and how to customize your résumé if you are in a special situation. This chapter will be of particular help if you are looking for your first job, if you are trying to change careers, or if you are returning to the work force after having been unemployed for awhile. You will see how to use the "Building Blocks" in different ways.

Chapter 6 is about how to write a covering letter, an essential part of each résumé. It also includes suggestions for keeping track of résumés you've sent.

In all of the chapters, plenty of models and examples are given.

The last chapter, *Chapter 7, "Beauty is in the Eyes of the Beholder,"* summarizes the advice given by the personnel officers who were interviewed for this book, and gives you their final check list for do's and don'ts.

A list of *Related Resources* at the end of the book provides ways and means of identifying recipients of your résumé.

Finally, you will find an *Appendix* of brief job descriptions. This will prove helpful to you in finding the right words and phrases for your résumé and in thinking of the specific job titles of jobs you might want to seek.

Building blocks

Build your winning résumé from pages and pages of your work, career goals, and life details that are then carefully selected and rephrased.

The first step in preparing your résumé is to gather the information that you have to work with. The purpose of this chapter is to help you gather and write down a great deal of information about yourself which may be useful to you in preparing your résumé. It is true that a brief, concise résumé is the most effective, and you will want to be sure that the final form of your résumé is not wordy, overdone, or long-winded. However, to begin with, you will need to take stock of all the experience, knowledge, and skills that you have to offer.

Consider Chapter 1 as your *information builder*. In each of the sections you will have a chance to jot down all the details you can think of. You will never use them all in the final version of your résumé; you will *choose* the details that are most applicable to the job you want. But before you can choose the best items to include, you will need to develop good, long lists of personal notes. Don't be afraid to write down a seemingly minor activity or accomplishment. If *you did it, you learned something from it,* and it may be useful. Put it down on paper, where you can look at it, and consider it as you build your résumé.

A winning résumé is built up step-by-step, using the elements which employers want to see quickly, and easily, as soon as they look at the résumé.

For the purposes of this book, we will call these elements *Blocks*—they are the *Building Blocks* of all résumés. These Building Blocks include all the kinds of information that employers need, in order to consider you for a job: information about your education and training, work history, and the like.

The first step in preparing your résumé is to gather information about yourself, and write it all down. Later, you will refine this information, boil it down, and rewrite it in the best wording, and the best order for the job you want to win.

Too many times, job applicants make the mistake of trying to write a rough draft of the whole résumé. They try to write *brief statements,* and never really look at all the experience they have had, and all the work they have done.

In this section you will explore and identify the key work experiences and accomplishments of your life. To do this, you will explore, through writing, all of the areas of your life that are related to work. The areas are as follows:

Block A: Education and training

Block B: Licenses and certificates

Block C: Work history

Block D: Related experience such as consulting, teaching or training others

Block E: Professional organizations, association memberships, and unions; committee memberships and offices held

Block F: Hobbies, community activities, volunteer work and leisure activities

Block G: Special abilities related to your work such as knowledge of a foreign language

Block H: Publications or presentations at meetings, conferences, or conventions

Block I: Skills assessment questionnaire

Before beginning work on this chapter, look over the list of Building Blocks. Remember that this book is written to help many people, each of whom has had a different set of experiences. If one of the Building Blocks has no meaning for you, do not try to force your life to fit the book: just skip that block! For example, if you are not active in community organizations, or if you have never made a speech or presentation, or published an article, ignore those pages and concentrate on the Building Blocks that can be used to show the experience that you have had. In the spaces given for your Personal Notes, you can jot down informally your own experiences.

Block A: Education and Training

> Concentrate on abilities, accomplishments, and energy you showed in school or college if you are a beginning worker.

Use this Building Block to identify your accomplishments in education. If you are looking for your first or second job, this section is very important in your résumé because this is the area in which you can show the ability and energy you have through the activities you took part in, in school. If you have been out of school, and working for a while, or are well advanced in your career, then you will probably just want to list any degrees you have earned, any special coursework which is of particular relevance to the job you are seeking, and any honors you have been awarded. If you have taken recent additional courses, those may be useful to include, as well.

Complete each of the sections below with attention to detail of names and dates. If you are uncertain of the dates or spelling of names, circle the item for research later. Then come back to fill in the missing information. In each section, begin with the most recent and work backwards into your past.

School History

In this section, you will list the names of all the schools you have attended, from high school to the present time. You may have only one school to list, or you may have several.

Keep in mind:

- All of your education is important to list.

- Start by listing your most recent schooling first.

- This list *is not the final form* for your résumé: it is for your own use.

Two examples of possible lists are included below to give you an idea of the kinds of schools you may want to list.

EXAMPLE

Name of School: New York University, New York, New York
Major or Area of Concentration: Business Administration
Degree or Credits Earned: Bachelor's Degree
Dates: September 1990–June 1994

EXAMPLE

Name of School: Price Academy of Business, Baltimore, Maryland
Major or Area of Concentration: Bookkeeping, Records Management
Degree or Credits Earned: None
Dates: September 1992–January 1993

Name of School: Parker High School, Baltimore, Maryland
Major or Area of Concentration: Accounting
Degree or Credits Earned: Diploma
Dates: September 1988–June 1992

Personal Notes

In the space below, write in all the school, college, and training programs you have completed. Be sure to write down *all* the educational background you have.

Name of School: _____

Major or Area of Concentration: _____

Degree or Credits Earned: _____

Dates: _____

Name of School: _____

Major or Area of Concentration: _____

Degree or Credits Earned: _____

Dates: _____

Name of School: _____

Major or Area of Concentration: _____

Degree or Credits Earned: _____

Dates: _____

Evidence of Knowledge

In this section you will want to think carefully of all the special courses or course content that you have had that might be of interest to the employer. If you were applying for a job as a carpenter, and you had also taken school courses in cabinet making, you would want to mention that special area of knowledge because it would qualify you for a broader field of jobs.

EXAMPLE

Course of Particular Interest: Systems Analysis
Relevance to Job: Seeking job in health services field. Field is increasingly computerized.

Personal Notes

Course of Particular Interest: _____

_____

Relevance to Job: _____

_____

Course of Particular Interest: _____

_____

Relevance to Job: _____

_____

Course of Particular Interest: _____

_____

Relevance to Job: _____

_____

Course of Particular Interest: _____

_____

Relevance to Job: _____

_____

Evidence of Independent Study   Many people neglect to mention special projects they have taken part in, where training may have contributed something of value to their educations or they revealed their energy or special skills. An employer may find that "something extra" in just such information. In this section, write down all the projects you have taken part in, on your own.

EXAMPLE

Special Projects and Papers: Worked on year-long project to aid elderly with nutritional needs.
Relevance to Job: Job requires skill with people of varied backgrounds.

Personal Notes

Special Projects and Papers: _____

_____

Relevance to Job: _____

_____

Special Projects and Papers: _____

_____

Relevance to Job: _____

_____

Special Projects and Papers: _____

_____

Relevance to Job: _____

_____

Special Projects and Papers: _____

_____

Relevance to Job: _____

_____

Evidence of Energy and Leadership

If you belonged to student or other organizations, held offices or led fund raising drives, these activities demonstrate your ability to take an active role in group activities. Jot down all those activities, to see which ones may apply when you write your résumé.

EXAMPLE

Organizations and Activities: Campus Daily Newspaper
Accomplishments: Served as business manager for two years.

Personal Notes

Organizations and Activities: _____

_____

Accomplishments: _____

_____

Organizations and Activities: _____

_____

Accomplishments: _____

_____

Organizations and Activities: _____

_____

Accomplishments: _____

_____

Organizations and Activities: _____

_____

Accomplishments: _____

_____

Honors   List here any awards, memberships in honorary societies, or special honors you have achieved. These might be strictly academic, or for some special achievement in sports, service clubs, or other activities. Be sure to include the name of the organization honoring you and the date of the award.

EXAMPLE

Honor: Dean's list, Baruch College, Academic Years 1991–92, 1992–93.

Personal Notes

Honor: _____

Awarding Organization: _____

Dates: _____

Honor: _____

Awarding Organization: _____

Dates: _____

Now that you have finished Block A, review your educational history and fill in any missing dates. Be sure that you check on the accuracy of any items you circled as uncertain. Ask friends, family members, or instructors to look over your notes to see if you have forgotten anything that might prove useful.

Block B: Certificates and Licenses

Use this section to record the data on any certificates or licenses required for the job you are seeking. If you have applied for a certificate, but have not yet received it, use the phrase, "application pending."

License requirements vary by state. If you have moved, or you are planning to move to a different state, check with the appropriate board or licensing agency in the state in which you are seeking work to be sure you know the requirements.

Be sure that all of the information listed is completely accurate. Locate copies of your licenses and certificates, check the dates and exact names of accrediting agencies.

EXAMPLE

Name of License: Teacher of English, Permanent
Licensing Agency: State of New Jersey, Department of Education
Date Issued: 1994

Personal Notes

Name of License: _____

Licensing Agency: _____

Date Issued: _____

Name of License: _____

Licensing Agency: _____

Date Issued: _____

Name of License: _____

Licensing Agency: _____

Date Issued: _____

Block C: Work History

> *Use your work history as the central focus of your résumé.*

This section will provide the central focus of your résumé. When your résumé is finished, the whole thing will be only one or two pages long. However, in filling out this block, it is important that you be as complete as possible. It is only by examining your experiences in depth, that you can get to the core of your accomplishments, and present them in a way that shows how strong your qualifications are. As you work, be aware of the need for accuracy. However, don't let a long search for a record that will tell you whether you left a job in May or June of 1978 distract you from the flow of self-examination and writing. When you are missing some detail, just circle that item and come back to it later.

Complete these sections in reverse chronological order as you did the items in *Block A: Education.* Begin with the most recent, and work backwards.

EXAMPLE

Job Title: Partner in charge of audits   **Dates:** 1990 to 1994
Employer: Martin and Company, Accountants
Address: 432 Madison Avenue
City, State, Zip: New York, NY 10017
Major Duties: Conducted audits of the following types of clients: public, multi-national, multi-plant manufacturing corporation; publishing company; investment advisory service; public housing and health services agencies. Prepared annual reports from clients to shareholders. Prepared corporate tax returns.
Special Projects: Helped clients in their selection of hardware and software for their internal accounting and bookkeeping systems. Utilized spreadsheet software in budgeting for clients and firm.
Evidence of Leadership: Was partner responsible for hiring in the firm. Initiated project to acquire and utilize word processors.
Evidence of Special Skills: I was frequently consulted by clients in their purchase of microcomputers. I wrote DBASE III programs to augment packaged software.
Company Accomplishments for Which I Was Responsible: Through automation, the company was able to serve 20% more clients without increased personnel or operating costs.

Personal Notes

Job 1

Job Title: _____   **Dates:** _____

Employer: _____

Address: _____

City, State, Zip: _____

Major Duties: _____

_____

_____

Special Projects: _____

_____

_____

Evidence of Leadership: _____

_____

Evidence of Special Skills: _____

_____

Company Accomplishments for Which I Was Responsible: _____

_____

_____

Job 2

Job Title: _____   **Dates:** _____

Employer: _____

Address: _____

City, State, Zip: _____

Major Duties: _____

_____

_____

Special Projects: _____

_____

_____

Evidence of Leadership: _____

_____

Evidence of Special Skills: _____

_____

_____

Company Accomplishments for Which I Was Responsible: _____

_____

_____

Job 3

Job Title: _____   **Dates:** _____

Employer: _____

Address: _____

City, State, Zip: _____

Major Duties: _____

_____

_____

Special Projects: _____

_____

_____

Evidence of Leadership: _____

_____

_____

Evidence of Special Skills: _____

_____

_____

Company Accomplishments for Which I Was Responsible: _____

_____

_____

Job 4

Job Title: _____ **Dates:** _____

Employer: _____

Address: _____

City, State, Zip: _____

Major Duties: _____

_____

_____

Special Projects: _____

_____

_____

Evidence of Leadership: _____

_____

_____

Evidence of Special Skills: _____

_____

Company Accomplishments for Which I Was Responsible: _____

_____

_____

Block D: Related Experience

In this section, you will review any experiences you have had, such as teaching or consulting, which are related to your work. Record any work you have done, whether paid work or volunteer, in which you helped others using skills or knowledge that are very similar to the skills and knowledge you use in your regular full-time employment.

Of course, if your regular full-time employment is teaching or consulting, then you would use the previous block, Block C: Work History, to record your experience. If you have done volunteer or community work that you feel is less directly related to your primary job, but which illustrates other skills, you may want to record that in Block F: Volunteer and Leisure Activities.

EXAMPLE

Job Title: Security Guard
Organization or Group Served: Morgan Township Baseball League
Dates: 1989–1991
Activities and Accomplishments: Trained parents of team members in handling parking lot and stadium security for summer season of games.

Personal Notes

Related Experience 1

Job Title: _____

Organization or Group Served: _____

Dates: _____

Activities and Accomplishments: _____

_____

Related Experience 2

Job Title: _____

Organization or Group Served: _____

Dates: _____

Activities and Accomplishments: _____

_____

Related Experience 3

Job Title: _____

Organization or Group Served: _____

Dates: _____

Activities and Accomplishments: _____

_____

Related Experience 4

Job Title: _____

Organization or Group Served: _____

Dates: _____

Activities and Accomplishments: _____

_____

Block E: Professional Associations

Use this section to record your activities in professional associations, unions and other similar organizations. Be accurate in your dates. Review your areas of interest and involvement as a reminder of organizations you may want to list. If you have not been involved in professional associations, simply leave this section blank and if you took part in special activities, or held any offices, be sure to jot those down, too.

EXAMPLE

Name of Organization: Nevada State Society of Cosmetologists
Activities, or Offices Held, with Dates: President, 1993–1994; Chairperson of Membership Committee, 1991–1992

Personal Notes

Name of Organization: _____

Activities or Offices Held, with Dates: _____

_____

Name of Organization: _____

Activities or Offices Held, with Dates: _____

_____

Name of Organization: _____

Activities or Offices Held, with Dates: _____

_____

Name of Organization: _____

Activities or Offices Held, with Dates: _____

_____

Block F: Volunteer and Leisure Activities

> **Demonstrate your skills and energies through volunteer work.**

Use this section to review and record any important activities that you have pursued outside of work. These activities should not only be the ones which bring you pleasure, but those in which you have demonstrated your skills or your energies. This is another area which helps you to look at your accomplishments and put them into words.

You may have helped your religious group raise money for a special project. In that case, you have developed skills in fund raising and managing a fund-raising team. Working for a political party in door-to-door voter campaigns or managing bake sales or rummage sales are all volunteer activities that demonstrate skill and energy.

If you are looking for your first job, or if you are a home-maker ready to enter or re-enter the paid work force, this block is a very important one for you.

EXAMPLE

Activity: Community center wall hanging project
Evidence of Skill: I organized over 200 people in the community to produce wall hangings for the community center. I solicited materials from local merchants who donated them free of charge.
Areas of Accomplishment: The community center had wall hangings. I was able to organize many people. I was able to sell an idea.

Personal Notes

Leisure Activity 1

Activity: _____

Evidence of Skill: _____

_____

_____

Areas of Accomplishment: _____

_____

_____

Leisure Activity 2

Activity: _____

Evidence of Skill: _____

_____

_____

Areas of Accomplishment: _____

_____

_____

Leisure Activity 3

Activity: _____

Evidence of Skill: _____

_____

_____

Areas of Accomplishment: _____

_____

_____

Leisure Activity 4

Activity: _____

Evidence of Skill: _____

_____

_____

Areas of Accomplishment: _____

_____

_____

Block G: Special Work-Related Abilities

In this section you can record any special abilities that you have. Think particularly of how these abilities are related to the job you are seeking.

Examples of abilities you might want to note in this section include: fluency in one or more foreign languages, familiarity with particular brands of computer hardware or software, security clearances, the ability to travel or to relocate.

EXAMPLE

Ability: Able to operate on both MS DOS and Macintosh platforms.

Personal Notes

Ability: _____

_____

Ability: _____

_____

Ability: _____

_____

Block H: Publications and Presentations

Use this section to record any articles you have written, professional papers you have had published, or any presentations you have made. In doing this, remember that your paper did not have to be published by a major publisher. It may have been published by your school or your company in its own magazine. Similarly, your presentation may have been before a school or local group, not before a large national crowd. All of these should be included.

In recording papers and presentations, underline the title of the publication. Use quotation marks around the title of an article or a presentation.

EXAMPLE OF AN ARTICLE

Title: "Employees Celebrate Bonus Year"
Journal or Organization: Harcourt Paint and Glass Company Magazine
Place: Denver, Colorado
Date: September, 1993.

EXAMPLE OF A PRESENTATION

Title: "Using Communications Devices"
Journal or Organization: Apple Computer User Group
Place: New York, NY
Date: November, 1994

Personal Notes

Title: _____

Journal or Organization: _____

Place: _____

Date: _____

Title: _____

Journal or Organization: _____

Place: _____

Date: _____

Title: _____

Journal or Organization: _____

Place: _____

Date: _____

Title: _____

Journal or Organization: _____

Place: _____

Date: _____

Title: _____

Journal or Organization: _____

Place: _____

Date: _____

Title: _____

Journal or Organization: _____

Place: _____

Date: _____

Block I: Skills Assessment

> See how your strengths relate to jobs that interest you.

In previous blocks, you looked at your personal history—in education, work, and other activities—to come up with a list of skills and accomplishments which will form the central core of your résumé. This block will help you examine your abilities more directly, in relationship to the jobs you want to apply for.

The Skills Assessment Questionnaire which follows consists of 16 items. Think about each skill listed. Decide whether this is a skill you possess, and if you would like to use it on a job. For example, the first skill listed deals with the ability to do continuous work, that is, the same tasks many times a day, working at a steady pace. Decide if you are able to do continuous work, ask yourself if you want to. If the answer to both questions is yes, mark Item 1, "yes." If you cannot do continuous work, or prefer not to, mark Item 1, "no."

After you answer the 16 questions, turn to the following Job Matching Section. You will then be able to use the job matching section in three ways:

1. to see which jobs match your strengths and interests.

2. to see what skills you have used to do the job you have been doing.

3. to identify jobs which require the same skills you have used in your previous job or jobs.

Specific directions for each of these uses will be given after the skills assessment questionnaire.

Skills Assessment Questionnaire*

1. *Continuous:*
   On some jobs you do the same tasks many times a day and you work at a steady pace. Is this type of work for you?

   _____ YES _____ NO

2. *Precise:*
   On some jobs there is little room for error so you must be very exact in your work. Is this type of work for you?

   _____ YES _____ NO

3. *Using Facts:*
   On some jobs you use factual information to decide what to do. Is this type of work for you?

   _____ YES _____ NO

4. *Working with Others:*
   On some jobs you must deal with many different people to get your work done. Is this type of work for you?

   _____ YES _____ NO

5. *Persuading:*
   On some jobs you talk with people to try to influence other people's actions or ideas. Is this type of work for you?

   _____ YES _____ NO

6. *Decision Making:*
   On some jobs you are responsible for making major decisions about projects, plans, and other people's duties. Is this type of work for you?

   _____ YES _____ NO

7. *Change:*
   On some jobs you must move often from one task to another and use several different skills. Is this type of work for you?

   _____ YES _____ NO

*The Skills Assessment Questionnaire is an adaptation of *Quest,* copyrighted by the National Career Information System, University of Oregon, 1988; used with their permission.

8. *Creative:*
   On some jobs you must express feelings and ideas in artistic ways. Is this type of work for you?

   _____ YES _____ NO

9. *Eye-Hand Coordination:*
   On some jobs you need to be very good at handling objects quickly as you see them. Is this type of work for you?

   _____ YES _____ NO

10. *Working with Fingers:*
    On some jobs you need to be able to do very precise work with your fingers. You need to work with small things very quickly and carefully. Is this type of work for you?

    _____ YES _____ NO

11. *Checking Accuracy:*
    On some jobs you need to be very accurate at reading or copying written materials. You have to be very good at things like proofreading numbers and words. Is this type of work for you?

    _____ YES _____ NO

12. *Use of Words:*
    On some jobs you need to be able to read and understand instructions easily. You have to express yourself very clearly in writing, or when talking with people. Is this type of work for you?

    _____ YES _____ NO

13. *Use of Numbers:*
    On some jobs you need to be able to work very quickly and accurately with numbers or measurements. Is this type of work for you?

    _____ YES _____ NO

14. *Catching on to Things:*
    On some jobs you need the ability to understand procedures and the reasonings behind them. You have to be very good at figuring out complicated things quickly and easily. Is this type of work for you?

    _____ YES _____ NO

15. *Seeing Detail:*
On some jobs you need to be able to tell slight differences in shapes of objects and lengths of lines. You have to be able to see detail in objects, pictures or drawings. Is this type of work for you?

_____ YES _____ NO

16. *Physical Activity:*
Jobs require different amounts of physical activity. On some jobs you need to be very active: climbing, lifting, carrying. Is this type of work for you?

_____ YES _____ NO

Job Matching Section

You can use the job matching section in three ways.

1. Use the job matching section to see which jobs match your strengths and interests.
Directions: Fill in the circles at the top of each page to match your "yes" answers to the Skills Assessment Questionnaire. This is your Skills Profile. The skills used in each job have already been filled in. Go down the page, job by job, and note the number of matches between your Skills Profile and each job's skills in the first column on the left. The job or jobs with the greatest number of matches come closest to your skills. You can see a brief description of jobs that interest you in Appendix C to this book.

2. Use the section to see what skills you have used to do the job you have been doing.
Directions: Skip down the list to the job title that comes nearest the job you have held. The skills for that job have already been filled in. These are the skills you used in carrying out that job successfully. Fill in these skills for yourself in the circles at the top of the page. Look over your answers to the Skills Assessment Questionnaire. You may have other skills which were not usually used in the job. Add these to your completed Skills Profile at the top of the page.

3. Use the sheet to identify jobs which require the same skills you have used in your previous job or jobs. *Directions:* Look down the list of job titles and identify the title or titles that come closest to jobs you have held. The skills for these jobs have already been filled in. Fill in the same circles in your Skills Profile. If you used a skill in a previous job, but prefer not to use it in a new job, do not fill in that circle. Go down the page, job by job, and note the number of matches between your Skills Profile and each job's skills in the first column on the left. The job or jobs with the greatest number of matches come closest to your skills. A checklist of jobs with brief descriptions is included in Appendix C to this book. The list provides job descriptions to help you clearly identify the work you could expect to do in each of these kinds of jobs.

Your Skills Profile →

Occupation	NUMBER OF MATCHES	1 CONTINUOUS	2 PRECISE	3 USING FACTS	4 WORKING WITH OTHERS	5 PERSUADING WITH OTHERS	6 DECISION MAKING	7 CHANGE	8 CREATIVE	9 EYE-HAND COORDINATION	10 WORKING WITH FINGERS	11 CHECKING ACCURACY	12 USE OF WORDS	13 USE OF NUMBERS	14 CATCHING ON TO THINGS	15 SEEING DETAIL	16 PHYSICAL ACTIVITY
Accountants & Auditors		•	•			•					•	•	•	•		
Administrators, Educational				•	•	•					•	•	•	•	•	
Administrators, Health Service				•		•	•				•	•	•			
Administrators, Public				•		•	•				•	•	•	•	•	
Agricultural Scientists			•			•				•		•	•	•		
Air Traffic Controllers		•	•			•	•				•	•	•			
Architects				•	•			•			•	•	•	•	•	
Biologists		•	•					•	•	•	•	•	•	•		
Bookkeepers		•					•	•	•		•	•	•	•	•	
Business Executives				•	•	•					•	•	•	•		
Buyers				•	•	•	•				•	•	•	•		
Chemists		•	•			•	•		•		•	•	•	•		
Chiropractors			•	•		•			•	•	•	•	•	•		•
Claims Adjusters & Examiners			•	•							•	•	•	•		
Commercial Artists								•	•	•	•	•	•	•	•	
Computer Operators			•				•		•	•	•	•	•	•	•	
Computer Programmers		•	•								•	•	•	•		
Computer Repairers		•	•	•		•	•		•		•	•	•	•		
Construction Superintendents				•		•	•				•	•	•	•		
Counselors			•	•			•				•	•	•			
Dental Hygienists		•		•				•	•		•	•	•	•		
Dentists		•	•	•	•		•			•	•	•	•	•		•
Designers, Clothes		•		•						•	•	•	•	•		
Designers, Floral			•				•	•	•	•	•	•	•	•		
Designers, Interior				•	•	•		•	•		•	•	•	•	•	
Dietitians			•	•		•					•	•	•			
Dispatchers	•		•								•		•	•		
Drafters		•	•					•	•	•	•	•	•	•		
Ecologists		•	•			•	•		•	•	•	•	•			
Economists			•			•					•	•	•	•		
Electricians		•	•				•		•	•	•	•	•	•	•	•
Engineers		•	•			•	•		•	•	•	•	•	•		
Financial Managers				•	•		•				•	•	•	•	•	
Fish & Wildlife Specialists			•				•		•	•			•			•

Your Skills Profile →

Column	Skill
1	CONTINUOUS
2	PRECISE
3	USING FACTS
4	WORKING WITH OTHERS
5	PERSUADING
6	DECISION MAKING
7	CHANGE
8	CREATIVE
9	EYE-HAND COORDINATION
10	WORKING WITH FINGERS
11	CHECKING ACCURACY
12	USE OF WORDS
13	USE OF NUMBERS
14	CATCHING ON TO THINGS
15	SEEING DETAIL
16	PHYSICAL ACTIVITY

(Leftmost wide column: NUMBER OF MATCHES)

	1	2	3	4	5	6	7	8	9	10	11	12	13	14	15	16
Foresters			●	●		●	●					●	●	●	●	
Geologists		●	●			●	●		●		●	●	●	●		
Graphic Artists							●	●	●	●	●	●	●	●		
Health & Safety Inspectors		●	●	●								●	●	●	●	
Hotel/Motel Managers			●		●	●					●	●	●	●		
Instrument Repairers		●	●						●	●	●	●	●	●		
Insurance Brokers			●	●	●				●	●	●	●	●	●		
Lawyers			●	●		●					●	●	●	●		
Legal Assistants		●	●	●		●					●	●	●	●		
Librarians			●			●					●	●	●	●		
Loan Officers			●	●							●	●	●	●		
Market Research Analysts			●	●							●	●	●	●		
Mathematicians		●	●								●	●	●	●		
Mechanics, Automobile		●	●				●		●	●	●	●		●	●	●
Mechanics, Heating & Cooling		●	●						●	●	●	●	●	●	●	●
Military Enlisted Personnel			●			●			●	●						●
Military Officers			●		●	●				●	●	●	●	●		
Nurses (LPN)		●		●		●			●	●		●		●	●	●
Nurses (RN)		●	●	●					●	●	●	●		●	●	●
Office Managers			●	●		●	●				●	●	●	●		
Opticians		●	●						●	●	●	●	●	●		
Optometrists			●	●					●	●	●	●	●	●		
Personnel Officers			●	●		●					●	●	●	●		
Pharmacists		●	●	●						●	●	●	●	●		
Photographers		●		●				●	●	●	●	●	●	●		
Physicians			●	●		●			●	●	●	●	●	●		
Physicists		●	●			●	●		●	●	●	●	●	●		
Pilots & Flight Engineers		●	●				●		●	●	●	●	●	●		
Production Managers			●			●	●				●	●	●	●		
Psychologists			●	●			●				●	●	●	●		
Public Relations Workers			●	●	●	●					●	●	●	●		
Purchasing Agents			●	●	●	●					●	●	●	●		
Quality Control Inspectors		●	●					●	●	●	●	●	●	●		
Radio & TV Broadcasters		●		●			●				●	●	●	●		
Real Estate Appraisers			●								●	●	●	●	●	
Real Estate Brokers				●	●						●	●	●	●	●	

Your Skills Profile →

Occupation	1 CONTINUOUS	2 PRECISE	3 USING FACTS	4 WORKING WITH OTHERS	5 PERSUADING	6 DECISION MAKING	7 CHANGE	8 CREATIVE	9 EYE-HAND COORDINATION	10 WORKING WITH FINGERS	11 CHECKING ACCURACY	12 USE OF WORDS	13 USE OF NUMBERS	14 CATCHING ON TO THINGS	15 SEEING DETAIL	16 PHYSICAL ACTIVITY
Receptionists	•			•							•	•		•		
Recreation Program Directors				•		•	•				•	•	•	•		
Salespersons				•	•				•		•	•	•	•		
Sales & Service Managers				•		•					•	•	•	•	•	
Sales Representatives				•	•						•	•	•	•		
Secretaries		•		•			•			•	•	•	•	•	•	
Social Scientists			•			•					•	•	•	•	•	
Social Workers				•	•	•					•	•	•			
Speech Pathologists				•					•	•	•	•	•	•		
Stockbrokers			•	•	•	•					•	•	•			
Surveyors		•	•			•			•	•	•	•	•			
Systems Analysts			•	•							•	•	•	•		
Teachers, Elementary & Secondary				•	•	•	•				•	•	•	•		
Teachers, Performing Arts				•	•	•	•	•			•	•	•	•		
Teachers, University & College				•	•	•					•	•	•	•		
Technicians, Broadcast		•	•						•	•	•	•	•	•		
Technicians, Dental Lab		•	•			•		•	•		•	•	•	•		
Technicians, Electronics		•	•				•		•	•	•	•	•	•	•	
Technicians, Emergency Medical			•	•					•	•	•	•	•	•		•
Technicians, Health		•	•	•					•	•	•	•	•	•	•	
Technicians, Medical Records		•		•			•				•					
Technicians, Nuclear Power		•	•				•				•	•	•	•	•	
Technicians, Radio & TV Service		•	•				•		•	•	•	•	•	•	•	
Therapists, Occupational				•			•			•	•	•	•	•		
Therapists, Physical		•	•	•	•	•			•	•	•	•	•	•		
Travel Agents				•	•						•	•	•			
Underwriters		•	•			•					•	•	•	•		
Urban & Regional Planners				•			•				•	•	•	•		
Veterinarians		•	•	•					•	•	•	•	•	•		•
Word Processing Machine Operators		•							•	•	•	•	•	•		
Writers & Editors				•	•				•	•	•	•	•	•	•	
Writers, Freelance									•		•			•		

Summary Worksheet

The purpose of this chapter has been to help gather all the information you need for a winning résumé. To do this, you had to examine key areas of your life so you could be more completely aware of your own skills and accomplishments.

One of the best ways to make a decision is first to look at all the possible options you have and then choose among them. Writing your résumé is a series of decisions about what to tell of your work-related experiences. This chapter helped you look at the possible details you *could* include. Later chapters will help you choose which to include.

Use the checklist below to review your options.

_____ I listed all degrees, the schools at which I earned them, and the dates I attended.

_____ I listed courses of particular relevance to the job I am seeking.

_____ I listed projects or papers I completed which show job-related accomplishments.

_____ I listed school organizations in which I showed leadership.

_____ I listed honors I had earned.

_____ I listed licenses and certificates I hold.

_____ I reviewed all my jobs and wrote down my duties, skills and accomplishments.

_____ I reviewed my experience and accomplishments in related activities, community activities, and professional organizations.

_____ I listed all papers and presentations I have given.

_____ I answered the Skills Assessment Questionnaire.

_____ I checked all dates, names and addresses.

> **Remember:**
>
> A winning résumé is built step by step using the elements that employers want to see quickly and easily.

Actions speak louder than words—use verbs

Employers who were interviewed for this book said that what impresses them most in a winning résumé is the forthright statement of what the job applicant has accomplished. The first thing that all the employers said they looked for was *what people had done in their previous work.* They all said that they were looking for *experience directly connected to the jobs they were trying to fill.*

In this section, you will take the statements you made about yourself in the "Building Blocks" and translate them into the words that your readers—people with the power to consider you for a job—are looking for. Two important techniques or methods are included.

The first technique involves taking your statements from sections of the building blocks and rephrasing them with *action words,* or *verbs.* The second technique involves your *translating your experiences into the language of job descriptions.*

Method 1: Using Action Words

Action words are verbs. One way to identify a verb is by the fact that it can usually take an "ed" ending to form the past tense. Another way to identify a verb is to try to use the word "I" in front of it. A checklist of verbs, in the past tense or "ed" form follows. Of course, these are not the only verbs you can use, nor will you be able to use all of them; but this list will offer very specific action words as models.

The first step is to look over the list of verbs that follows. Mentally put the word "I" in front of them. See if the verb fits a specific action or accomplishment of yours. If it does, put a pencil check next to it, or circle it, for use later.

List of Verbs

administered
advised
analyzed
arranged
assembled
assumed responsibility
billed
built
carried out
channeled
collected
communicated
compiled
completed
conducted
contacted
contracted
coordinated
counseled
created
cut
designed
determined
developed
directed
dispatched
distributed
documented
edited
established
expanded
functioned as
gathered
handled
hired

implemented
improved
inspected
interviewed
introduced
invented
maintained
managed
met with
motivated
negotiated
operated
orchestrated
ordered
organized
oversaw
performed
planned
prepared
presented
produced
programmed
published
purchased
recommended
recorded
reduced costs
referred
represented
reviewed
saved
screened
served as
served on
sold

suggested   trained
supervised   typed
taught   was promoted
tested   wrote

Rewriting Your Work   Review the statements you made in the work history sec-
History   tion and rewrite them to stress your actions, that is, use a
verb to begin each statement.

Look over your work history for Job 1, your most recent,
perhaps your present, job. Look at all the parts of that job
description that you wrote: Major Duties, Special Projects,
Evidence of Leadership, Evidence of Special Skills, and
Company Accomplishments. Now translate that information into actions, using the verbs previously listed (and any
others that you need).

EXAMPLE FROM BUILDING BLOCK C

This is information that was recorded by one résumé writer in a Work History Block:
Job Title: Attorney
Employer: Self-employed
Major Duties: Diversified legal and tax practice. Outside counsel for ABC Title Co.
Representative for accountants and their clients before the IRS and tax courts.
Closer for several title companies.
Special Projects: Coordinator and co-sponsor of a semi-annual seminar for newly
admitted attorneys.
Evidence of Leadership: Managed own practice.
Evidence of Special Skills: Adjunct Professor of Law and Taxation at Brooklyn
Law School.
Company Accomplishments for which I was Responsible: All

This is the rewritten version, using verbs. As you read
it, hear how much stronger it sounds.

REWRITTEN EXAMPLE

Developed and directed diversified law and tax practice. Served as outside counsel to
ABC Title Co. Conducted closings for several title companies. Represented clients
and accountants before the Internal Revenue Service and Tax Courts. Coordinated
and sponsored a semi-annual seminar for newly admitted attorneys. Taught courses
in Law and Taxation, as adjunct professor, at Brooklyn Law School.

As you read this, you can see that this writer decided to include teaching experience in the work history. If the writer had wished, he or she could have put that in the section for "Related Experience."

Now turn back to your Work History in Block C of Chapter 1 and rewrite each job description, beginning each statement with a verb. You can use the word "I" before each verb if you prefer.

Personal Notes

Job 1: Action Description: _____

_____

_____

_____

Job 2: Action Description: _____

_____

_____

_____

Job 3: Action Description: _____

_____

_____

_____

Job 4: Action Description: _____

_____

_____

_____

Rewriting Other Building Blocks

As you look over your personal history in the building blocks, you may realize that the strongest expression of your accomplishments is not in your work history, but in other areas. For example, if you are a beginning worker, your strongest accomplishments may have been in school activities. If you are trying to change careers, the most relevant experience to the new job you are seeking may have been in activities recorded in "Related Experience." If you have been a homemaker, the best expression of your skills may have been those recorded in Block F: Volunteer and Leisure Activities. All of the accomplishments and skills you recorded in those Building Blocks can and should be rewritten in the action form.

Review the list of verbs at the beginning of this section. Again, make a check next to those that you can identify with. Now go back to the Building Blocks that you completed and rewrite them in the sections provided next.

EXAMPLE FROM BUILDING BLOCK A

This example is from the Building Blocks notes of a new worker. Almost all of this applicant's experience has been in school.

Organizations and Activities: *Phoenix* (college paper)
Accomplishments: The paper was redesigned while I was managing editor. I organized a new system for reporters' assignments. I also reported all student government events before I was editor.

REWRITTEN EXAMPLE

This is the rewritten version using verbs:

Served as Managing Editor for two years, and before that as reporter. Redesigned layout of the paper. Organized and implemented an improved beat reporting system. Covered all student government events.

EXAMPLE FROM BUILDING BLOCK F

This example is from the résumé of a homemaker whose major accomplishments are in volunteer activities:

Activity: Franklin Avenue Church, chair of finance committee
Areas of Accomplishment: Responsible for day-to-day operations of the church's finances, including maintenance of accounting records, payment of bills and bank reconciliations. Report frequently to church leadership and periodically to congregation. Correspond and meet with attorneys. Prepare financial statements for review by court. Currently supervising and training staff of five committee members.

REWRITTEN EXAMPLE

This is the rewritten statement, stressing action:

Managed all church finances. Maintained accounting records and prepared financial statements for review by court. Reconciled statements. Prepared and delivered oral and written reports to the church leadership and congregation. Corresponded and met with attorneys on behalf of church. Trained and supervised volunteer staff.

Personal Notes

Now rewrite information from the Building Blocks that are important to your history in the spaces provided below.

Action Rewrite 1: _____

_____

_____

_____

Action Rewrite 2: _____

_____

_____

_____

Action Rewrite 3: _____

_____

_____

_____

Action Rewrite 4: _____

_____

_____

_____

Method 2: Using Job Descriptions

Every job and industry has a special *vocabulary*, or *jargon*, a way of using words, that is special to that field. Another way of catching and holding the interest of the reader of your résumé is to use the words the reader expects to see.

In Appendix C you will find 100 job descriptions. Each job description contains a paragraph describing job responsibilities in specific, generally accepted terms which are in common use by corporations, government employment organizations, and other modern business institutions and another listing the skills and aptitudes required. Use the job descriptions to rewrite the material in your Building Blocks so that it captures the language of the job and field that interest you. This method of rewriting your personal history is particularly useful if you are trying to change careers, enter the job market for the first time, or develop a "portfolio career." A portfolio career enables you to take advantage of all your skills, talents, and abilities, in a variety of part-time, contractual, and consulting jobs. You can use the same experience expressed in different words to attract varied potential employers.

Another source of job descriptions is the *Occupational Outlook Handbook* which describes virtually all the thousands of the jobs in the United States. You may also want to look at one or more of the numerous books about specific fields such as *Careers in Communications, Careers in High Tech, Opportunities in Plastics Careers, Opportunities in Customer Service Careers* or *Careers for Bookworms and Other Literary Types.* These are just a few of the hundreds of titles available to you in your library or bookstore.

In your library, school, university, or employment service office, you may also have access to a computer-based career information delivery system. These systems contain up-to-date descriptions of hundreds of occupations as well as helpful information on related training.

Finally, don't forget about the companies that you are considering in your job search. Some organizations make information such as job descriptions available for the asking. Call the personnel or human resource development office.

EXAMPLE FROM BUILDING BLOCK C

This example is from the résumé of a recent college graduate. While she was in college, she held a summer job as a supervising field interviewer for a citizens' action group. This is what she wrote in her original Building Block.

I helped citizens become aware of the state legislative process and issues of toxic waste, utility control and consumer legislation. I helped the field interviewers communicate better with the citizens. I was responsible for developing and maintaining motivation among the employees, and for supervising their work.

EXAMPLE OF A JOB DESCRIPTION

This is the job description for Public Administrator:

Responsibilities: Coordinate and direct public services to meet the needs of the nation, state, or community. Analyze problems; work with special committees and public agencies; recommend solutions to governing bodies.

Aptitudes and Skills: Ability to relate to and communicate with people; solve complex problems through analysis; plan, organize, and implement policies and programs. Knowledge of political systems; financial management; personnel administration; program evaluation; organizational theory.

REWRITTEN EXAMPLE

This is the rewritten description of the same accomplishments.

Wrote pamphlets and conducted discussion groups to inform citizens of legislative processes and consumer issues. Organized and supervised crew of interviewers. Trained interviewers in effective communication skills.

EXAMPLE OF ANOTHER JOB DESCRIPTION

An individual with the same background looking for a first job as a purchasing agent or an assistant to a purchasing agent could rewrite the same experience differently. Here is the job description:

Responsibilities: Buy merchandise, materials, supplies and equipment needed for an organization to function. Analyze needs; develop and write specifications; negotiate with salespeople.

Aptitudes and Skills: Ability to work on details; to work with people; to work easily with numbers; to write clear product specifications. Knowledge of purchasing practices; of contract, property, and insurance laws; of supplies; of pricing methods and discounts; of inventory control; of finance; of accounting.

REWRITTEN EXAMPLE

Here is the rewritten version of the same experience, tailored to fit the job description for a purchasing agent:

Organized team of field workers to promote citizen awareness of laws relating to consumer affairs. Trained interviewers in techniques for clear oral communication. Wrote specific directions for conducting interviews.

Rewriting Your Building Blocks

Rewrite your Building Blocks using the job descriptions at the back of this book. In doing this, remember to continue to use the action words discussed and listed in Method 1 of this chapter.

Job Related Rewrite 1: _____

_____

_____

Job Related Rewrite 2: _____

_____

_____

Job Related Rewrite 3: _____

_____

_____

Job Related Rewrite 4: _____

_____

_____

As you look over your action and job-related statements, you may feel they sound simple. Resist any impulse to change that simplicity. All of the personnel officers interviewed pulled many résumés from their files to show us statements that were so grand, they were laughable. Some examples of statements that are overdramatic or too grand will give you the idea: "A complete conceptualization with practical realization," and, "Developed keen dexterity with the panoply of tax research materials." A winning résumé may evoke a smile of empathy and recognition, but it shouldn't produce a belly laugh!

Summary Worksheet

The purpose of this chapter was to help you rewrite your work and work-related experiences into the language that has the most effect in a résumé.

Winning résumés use verbs to convey a strong sense of action, and also use specific vocabulary associated with the job being sought.

Use the checklist below to review.

_____ I reviewed the list of verbs on pages 33 and 34 and used as many as I could.

_____ I added some verbs to the list and used them in describing my experiences.

_____ All my experience is described in terms of action, in terms of what I did.

_____ I also rewrote the description of student activities, related experience, or volunteer work using verbs.

_____ I read the job description or descriptions that apply to my work in Appendix C.

_____ I used language from the job descriptions to highlight my skills and accomplishments at work.

_____ I kept all my rewritten descriptions simple and to the point.

Remember:

To build a winning résumé, you need to begin by taking stock of *all* the experience, knowledge, and skills that you have to bring to a new job. Too many people try to begin by writing a brief statement, and never really look at all they have to offer.

Assembly

3

Know what to include and what to leave out for a winning résumé.

This chapter will help you assemble all the parts you have prepared in the last two sections. First you will examine all of the essential parts of the résumé and be sure that you have the necessary information for them. Then, you will take a look at the optional portions and decide which of those you would like to include. The third part of this chapter consists of sample résumés. Look them over to get a picture of how your résumé may look. Finally, an outline is provided to help you draft your own résumé.

Essential Parts of a Résumé
Heading

This section, which will go at the top of your résumé, will include your name, home address, and telephone numbers. If you can receive calls at work, include your business number. This makes it easier for people to reach you during their business day.

Education

This section will include the information from Building Block A. If you are an experienced worker, include the degrees you have earned, the institutions at which you earned them and the dates of attendance. List your most advanced degree first. If you have recently taken courses to upgrade or enhance your skills, include these also. Finally, if you were awarded any honors in school, these are still yours! Include them.

If you are not an experienced worker, include any unusual or particularly significant coursework or special projects or papers that you did. The purpose of this is to show a high level of energy and/or accomplishment. If you took the regular course of study for your field, do not list your courses. One of the worst résumé-writing sins all of the employers cited was the desire to puff oneself up and to make the ordinary seem rare.

Work History

Include here the information from Building Block C and the rewritten action and job-related descriptions from Chapter 2. For each job, be sure to give your job title, your employer's name and address, and the dates of employment. Be direct and to the point. Be sure to list your most recent experience first. In general, you will also give more spaces to a description of your duties and accomplishments in your most recent position as well.

You will have to decide how to include company accomplishments: a good rule to follow is to include only those for which you were directly responsible. One of the personnel officers interviewed said, "It's really a turn-off when people claim full credit for achievements they were associated with, rather than those they did wholly on their own."

According to our experts, it is better *not* to include your reasons for leaving your last job on your résumé. While this is important information, it is better to discuss the matter during the interview.

If you are just out of school, do show summer and part-time employment.

Professional Licenses and Certificates

This section is included if licensure or certification is required in your field. The license, issuing agency, and date of issuance should be included. This section goes immediately before, or immediately after, your work history. See Building Block B for details.

Optional Sections

The following sections are optional. As you read the descriptive material, you will see suggestions as to whether or not you should include them. In deciding, bear in mind that all the people interviewed said that conciseness and brevity were important to them in reviewing a résumé. Your goal—the winning résumé—should be a résumé that is one or, at most, two pages long.

Related Experience

If you have work experience that does not fall neatly into your work history, this is a convenient way to show it without confusing the chronology of your résumé. Look back at Building Block D to make this decision.

Professional Association Memberships and Offices Held

Only you know whether you have significant accomplishments in this sphere of activity. In most fields, work in professional associations is considered a plus in your portfolio of experience. If you filled in information in Building Block E, list that information on your résumé. If your résumé is getting too long, you can summarize this and just list recent highlights.

Leisure Activities

This is another truly optional section. Look over the accomplishments you listed in Block F. If you feel that what you have done in your hobbies, community activities, or volunteer work reflects energy or accomplishments that you would like the hiring official to see, include them. Remember, however, that these do not generally substitute for solid accomplishment in work, no matter how important they may have been to you or to others. If this is your main area of accomplishment, you will want to look closely at the chapter on customizing your résumé. Some of the employers interviewed said that they paid no attention to this section. Others said they liked to use it to engage an applicant in conversation. (If you include any activities, you had better be prepared to talk about them. Don't try to fake it!) Still others said they thought anyone who listed hobbies needed something to fill the page. The final line of advice on leisure activities is: If you have some serious area of interest in which you have demonstrated skills or accomplishments, list it. If you have no hobbies or only passing interests, leave this section out.

Special Abilities

If you have special abilities that are valuable in your work, be sure to list them. In the computer field, these knowledges and abilities go at the start of the résumé, before education. In other fields, they generally follow work history. Look back at Block G.

Publications and Presentations

In completing Block H, you saw how to detail your publications and presentations. These should be included. If you happen to have written many publications, and you fear a list will make your résumé too long, make a simple statement within the résumé, and then attach a list at the end. If this section does not apply to your accomplishments, simply omit it.

Stating Your Job Objective

There is varied opinion on the inclusion of a job objective. Some employers prefer to see it, and others see it as an item that belongs in the cover letter.

If you have a specific job objective within a field, such as tax accountant, or computer operator, then the objective may be included on the résumé or in the cover letter. If you are open to many jobs, do not include an objective like: "a challenging position in a company with growth possibilities." This is taken for granted and does not tell the prospective employer anything new. Have you ever heard of anyone who wanted a boring position in a company destined to go nowhere? If you do not have a specific job objective, or if the objective cannot be reduced to a single clear phrase, then omit this section. Use your cover letter to state your job objective, and state it in terms related to the job you are applying for.

Summary or Highlights

The consensus among employers is that a "summary" or "highlights" section is not needed on a résumé. Some of the hiring officials interviewed said that they did not care whether it was there or not, others said they preferred not to see it. One said, "I like to draw my own conclusions." Another said, "No highlights—that's what a whole résumé should be. If you have to summarize the résumé, you have too much in there."

Age, Marital Status, and Physical Characteristics

These were the résumé items on which there was the greatest variation among employers interviewed. There were, in general, two schools of thought. The first school, in favor of including these items, said things like: "It doesn't matter to me, but I like to get a picture of a person when I read about her or him," and "It helps me see if a person will fit into a group of people I already have." The second group, those not in favor, said things like: "We are trained not to look at that," and "Don't include these items. It's illegal to discriminate on the basis of age or marital status anyway."

What should you do? Your goal is to write a winning résumé. If you believe that your personal characteristics are right on target for the job you are seeking, include them. If you have any doubts, leave them out. For example, if you are looking for an upper level executive position, stability is generally considered important, and being married may be considered a mark of stability by the interviewer. If you are married with two children, include that fact. On the other hand, if you are looking for a middle management job, and you think that a hiring company may see your spouse and children as a liability because they would inhibit your readiness for relocation, leave them out. In general: if in doubt, leave this section out!

In no way is falsification suggested here. Throughout your résumé writing, simple statements of the facts are essential. However, you are the judge of which facts to include. You can't put everything into the résumé. Remember, *if your résumé wins, it does not get you a job: it gets you an interview.* At that time, it is up to the person interviewing you to find out all the company wants and needs to know.

References

The employers did not expect to see a list of references in a résumé, but they found it helpful when it was there. One expert who found it most helpful had been in the field for many years. He said, "I know so many people in the field. I like to pick up the phone and get the true story." If you have references of people directly involved in your field, you may want to list them.

Sample Résumés   On the next few pages, you will find some good sample résumés. Look them over for ideas. Be sure to notice the use of action words, the direct relationship of experience to the work the applicant is hoping for. Then go to the end of this chapter to draft your own résumé.

These are actual résumés of real people's work experience and backgrounds. The names, addresses, and telephone numbers have been fictionalized to protect the privacy of the people who wrote them.

Your own résumé will be uniquely your own, but it will include patterns that are similar to one or more of the sample résumés. As you write your rough draft of your résumé, don't be afraid to try out different wording. Write and rewrite your descriptions, and look at several different forms to see what wording you like best.

RÉSUMÉ

Jose Emanuel

Residence: 3300 N. Dodge
Omaha, Nebraska 68130
(402) 330-7749

Office: 1800 W. Maple
Omaha, Nebraska 68114
(402) 397-2540

DRAFTER

<u>Job Objective</u>—To be employed as a drafter with a large company.

<u>Professional Experience</u>
Drafter—1990 to present

Quewit Manufacturers, Omaha, Nebraska

Duties cover completing projects on three schools, a library, a shopping mall and other public sites.

<u>Educational Background</u>
Technical Community College, Bellvue, Nebraska, enrolled in evening computer programming course (at present), expect a B.S. in 1995

Mechanics Institute, Lincoln, Nebraska, drafting curriculum, 1988–1990

North High School, Omaha, Nebraska, 1984–1988

<u>Interests</u>
School Board No. 2, Member Curriculum Committee 1993-present

All sports, mountain climbing, photography.

<u>Personal</u>
Born: May 17, 1970, in Hastings, Nebraska
Height: 6'0"
Weight: 200
Status: Single
Health: Good

STEPHEN ROBBINS
FERRY ROAD
BRISTOL, RHODE ISLAND 02809
(401) 373-4662

EDUCATION:

UNIVERSITY OF RHODE ISLAND
Bachelor of Business Administration
Expected Date of Graduation: August 1994
MAJOR: Accounting—CPA Preparation
GPA in Major: 3.3/4.0
GPA Overall: 3.0/4.0

WORK EXPERIENCE:
January 1992 to present

ROSE & WANG, CPAs Providence, Rhode Island
Staff Accountant:
—Prepared tax returns for corporations, partnerships,
  trusts, and individuals;
—Prepared clients' books and firm's workpapers for IRS tax
  audits;
—Organized and completed final workpaper schedules;
—Reviewed final financial statements for qualitative and
  quantitative errors;
—Footed totals of lines and columns on various supporting
  schedules.

January 1989 to
December 1991

MAKO BEARINGS INC. Providence, Rhode Island
Promoted to Assistant Branch Manager:
—Compiled stock orders to replace depleted inventories;
—Created system of internal controls for branch office;
—Authorized purchase orders for all back-ordered items;
—Collected receivables past due 60 days via telephone and
  mail correspondences;
—Determined pricing structure and published price list;
—Planned and implemented promotional sales campaign.
Order Clerk:
—Received incoming orders;
—Matched receiving reports to purchase orders, verifying
  accuracy;
—Acquired quotations from various vendors to fill back-
  ordered items.

SPECIAL SKILLS:

COMPUTER
—Able to program in DBASE III and C
—Academic courses in systems design and EDP Auditing;
—Practical experience with automated accounting systems.

REFERENCES FURNISHED UPON REQUEST

Gail Freeborne
30 Spear Street
Piscataway, New Jersey 08854
(201) 469-2814

Experience
JUNE 92–PRESENT   PROMOTIONAL WRITER/EDITOR/PROOFREADER
Sea Otter Press
New Brunswick, New Jersey
Duties include: Writing press releases to promote readings,
workshops, and benefits; editing manuscript submissions;
proofreading promotional materials; organizing activities.

SEP 91–MAY 92   ENGLISH TUTOR
Office of Alternatives for Individual Development
Rutgers College
Tutored rhetoric and literature to referral students at the Col-
lege.

SEP 90–MAY 92   NEWSPAPER REPORTER
Voice of the Students
Rutgers College
Reported campus news at the College.

SEP 90–MAY 91   PROMOTIONAL WRITER/PROOFREADER
Office of Community Services
Rutgers College
Wrote press releases to promote academic programs, guest
lecturers, special workshops, and athletic events; wrote educational advertisements; proofread galleys set for print; rewrote assigned material; filed and typed.

Other
Experience   SHIPPER/RECEIVER; MAIL CLERK; SUBSTITUTE
TEACHER; PSYCHIATRIC AID; LANDSCAPER; WAITER;
COOK.

Education
SEP 88–MAY 92   Rutgers College, Rutgers University
New Brunswick, New Jersey
Bachelor of Arts—English

NEAL J. MCKINLAY

P.O. Box 3892   Business: (503) 484-4757
Eugene, Oregon 97403   Residence: (503) 686-5093

EXPERIENCE

PHILIP & CO.   Portland, Oregon   1988 to Present

<u>Assistant Tax Director/Senior Tax Counsel</u> Responsible for tax research and tax plan-
ning, making recommendations and implementing them.

- Recruited, organized and trained a professional staff of seven capable of providing effective and timely tax planning guidance.
- Increased the short and long term utilization of foreign tax credits in the U.S.
- Analyzed, proposed and coordinated numerous domestic and foreign corporate reorganizations. Reviewed capital transactions of foreign subsidiary operations. Reviewed interaffiliate and third party licensing of intangibles.

MERITRON CORP.   Eugene, Oregon   1982–1988

<u>Tax Manager</u> Responsible for research and planning, advising management of tax op-
portunities.

- Reviewed U.S. consolidated tax return: prepared worldwide tax provision, handled IRS and state audits, and drafted ruling requests and protests.
- Responsible for research and planning in foreign tax credit utilization, subpart
  F income, foreign personal holding companies, tax haven operations, Section
  482, consolidated return regulations, reorganizations and liquidations.

PROFESSIONAL AFFILIATIONS

Attorney-at-Law admitted to practice in Oregon (1980)
C.P.A. admitted to practice in Oregon (1983)
Tax Executives Institute
International Tax Association
American and Oregon Bar Associations
American and Oregon Societies of C.P.A.s

EDUCATION

LL.M.   University of Oregon, Graduate Law Division (1989), major in Taxation
M.B.A.   University of Oregon Graduate School of Business Administration (1982),
           major in Accounting
J.D.   Stanford University Law School (1979), Stanford University Scholarship
B.A.   University of Oregon (1976), major in American Civilization, Dean's List,
           Junior Achievement Scholarships

Martin Diamond
1342 11th Avenue
San Francisco, California 94122

Home Telephone: 566-2489   Office Telephone: 720-4100

HARDWARE: IBM 4341/30XX
SOFTWARE: CICS Command Level, VSAM, VM/CMS, OS/MVS
LANGUAGES: COBOL, BAL

EXPERIENCE

Estimable Life Insurance Company   1984–present
San Francisco, California

Project Leader   1990–present
   Developed systems including: Deficiency Reserve Evaluation; Mortality and Termination Experience Studies, Agent Performance Analysis and Retirement Plan and Bonuses.
   Led a team of programmers and consultants to develop and implement the company's reinsurance systems including conversion, maintenance, automatic billing, on-line transaction generation, policy exhibit and management reports.
   Implemented LIFE-COMM version of Tax and STAT Reserve Valuation. Supervised a team of 15 professionals.

Senior Programmer/Analyst   1986–1990
   Developed and implemented company's declared dividend scale calculation, update and dividend liability systems.
   Improved and maintained actuarial, reinsurance, and general agents commission payment systems.
   Converted premium rates, cash values, reserve and dividends to LIFE-COMM systems.

Programmer/Analyst   1984–1986
   Responsible for various projects designed to calculate premium rates, values, reserves, and dividends.
   Developed general agents commission payment system.
   Participated in developing new product premium rates, cash values and dividends.

EDUCATION

San Francisco State College, B.S. (cum laude), 1984, Major: mathematics;
   Minor: computer systems.

The Résumé: First Draft

Using the outline provided in the next few pages, create a first draft of your résumé. Use the material you developed in the Building Blocks and the Action and Job-Related Rewrites. Use the ideas you got from looking over the sample résumés. In the outline, you will see space for all of the optional sections. Before including any of these, you may want to re-read the notes on optional sections given earlier in this chapter.

In the outline, headings which should be part of the finished product are in bold type, for example: **Education**. Items which are to be filled in *by you*, eliminating the word as a heading, are indicated by parentheses, for example: (Name). All *optional* items are marked with an asterisk, for example: Age*. To review the reasons for including one or more of the optional sections see pages 45 to 47.

Personal Notes

First Draft Résumé Form

(Name) _____

(Address) _____

(City, State, Zip Code) _____

(Home Telephone) _____

(Office Telephone) _____

Objective* _____
(State a job objective only if it is specific.)

Education (*Put this at the end of your résumé if you are an experienced worker.*)

(Diploma, Certificate or Degree) _____ (Dates) _____

(Institution) _____

(Major or Area of Concentration) _____

(Diploma, Certificate or Degree) _____ (Dates) _____

(Institution) _____

(Major or Area of Concentration) _____

Experience

(Job Title) _____ (Dates) _____

(Employer) _____

(Duties and Accomplishments) _____

_____

_____

(Job Title) _____ (Dates) _____

(Employer) _____

(Duties and Accomplishments) _____

_____

_____

_____

(Repeat as needed on scrap paper. Be sure to list your most recent experiences first and work backwards.)

Licenses and Certification

(License) _____ (Dates) _____

(Issuing Agency) _____

(License) _____ (Dates) _____

(Issuing Agency) _____

Related Work Experience*

(Job Title) _____ (Dates) _____

(Employer) _____

(Duties and Accomplishments) _____

_____

_____

(Repeat as often as needed.)

Honors*

_____

_____

Interests and Hobbies*

_____

_____

Special Abilities*

_____

_____

(List fluency in foreign languages, availability for travel, etc.)

Publications and Presentations*

_____

_____

Personal Information*

   Age: _____

   Height: _____ **Weight:** _____

   Health: _____

   Marital Status: _____

Summary Worksheet

The purpose of this chapter has been to help you choose the experiences and details that best show your educational and work history and your skills and accomplishments.

In Chapter 1 you wrote out and reviewed everything you could possibly use in your résumé. In this chapter you made the hard decision about what to include and what to leave out.

Use the checklist below to review your decisions.

_____ I have included information for the essential parts of a résumé.

    _____ Heading (Name, Address, Telephone Number)

    _____ Education

    _____ Work History

    _____ Certificates and Licenses

_____ I have read the information about optional sections.

_____ I have thought about my own experience and the job I am applying for, in deciding about including optional sections.

_____ I have included optional sections which show something strong in my experience.

_____ I have left out optional sections which would just be page fillers.

_____ I have a first draft of my résumé.

_____ I have compared it to one or more of the sample résumés.

_____ I have added or taken out some information.

_____ I like my résumé so far.

Remember:

The most impressive information on a winning résumé is the description of what the applicant has accomplished on previous jobs. Hiring officials are looking for experience directly connected with the jobs they are trying to fill.

Getting physical

> *Use the layout of your résumé to draw attention to its most important facts.*

In this chapter, you will use the draft of your résumé, which you created in the last chapter, and produce a finished copy. First, we will discuss ideas on layout and spacing. Then suggestions on typing, paper, and reproduction are provided. Finally, there is a section to help you with proofreading your résumé.

The personnel officers and hiring officials interviewed for this book stated clearly that there is no one style or paper that is preferable. What emerged from their comments is the *overwhelming importance of neatness and "good grooming" in a résumé*. Some of the worst sins that they objected to in résumé presentation are: sloppiness, misspellings, thumb smudges, hand corrections, whiting-out. One employer summed it up this way, "A piece of paper that has not been taken care of shows disdain for the reader, the process, and the job applicant himself." Others said that, since attention to detail was important to their fields, lack of attention to details in the résumés showed them that the applicants could probably not do the job at hand.

Organization that is easy to read and clarity of presentation are the two other factors to consider in preparation.

Layout   There is no single appropriate layout that will fit every résumé, but there are some good rules to follow.

First, leave at least a one-inch margin all around the page to frame the information.

Second, use spacing between lines and indentations of material to draw attention to important facts. Do not cram everything together.

Third, be consistent in the type of headings you use. For example, if you capitalize the heading EDUCATION, do not use initial capital letters and underlining for the equal heading, Job Experience.

Finally, try to fit your résumé onto one page. If this is not possible, try to arrange your material so that the most important items appear on page one.

All of the résumés given as examples in Chapter 3 are also examples of *good layouts*. Following are three examples of résumés with *poor layouts*. As you examine each résumé, try to identify the major layout errors.

EXAMPLE: PROBLEM RÉSUMÉ NO. 1

PAUL C. MICHAELS

2121 Sumac Street
Champaign, Ill. 61821

Messages &
Home: (217)
854-0852
854-1457

Business:
(217)
686-8400
Ext. 304

Auditor
Building Service Pension & Health Funds
Chicago, Illinois
September, 1991–Present
Responsibility: Autonomous audits
of contributing employers
Wang word processing experience.

Analyst
FairViews
Chicago, Illinois
May, 1990–Present
(Hobby)

M.B.A.
Seton Hall University, So. Orange, N.J. 07079
January, 1989–May, 1990
G.P.A.: 3.57
Concentration: Quantitative Analysis

Accountant
Bandlor–Hall, Inc.
Chicago, Illinois
September, 1985–January, 1989
Charges: Computerized financial statements,
bank reconciliations and journal entries.

B.S.
Seton Hall University, May, 1987
1983–December, 1986
Major: Accounting
Minor: Journalism

Accounting Clerk
Building Service Pension & Health Funds
Summers 1982–1990
Various bookkeeping duties.

References will be furnished upon request.

EXAMPLE: PROBLEM RÉSUMÉ NO. 2

MARK E. RUCZINSKI
4330 Chesapeake NW
Washington, D.C. 20010

PERSONAL:

Born: May 10, 1958
Married with two children

Height 6'2"
Weight 160 lbs.

EDUCATION:

1986–1988   Pace University School of Law, White Plains, New York

J.D. Received June 1989

1982–1984   Iona College Graduate School of Business New Rochelle, New York

Masters degree in Business Administration in Accounting, received in June 1984

1973–1980   Iona College New Rochelle, New York

Bachelor of Business Administration received in Finance June 1973; member of Dean's Honor List, last four semesters; Received scholarship to Iona College Graduate School of Business.

PROFESSIONAL QUALIFICATIONS:

Admission to New York Bar—1989
Certified Public Accountant—New York 1985
Member of the American Institute of Certified Public Accountants
Member of the New York Society of Certified Public Accountants

BUSINESS EXPERIENCE:

1987 To Present   Greyhound Bus Lines, Inc. New York New York

Assistant General Counsel and Assistant to Treasurer

Responsibilities include, tax research and planning for the corporation and its subsidiaries, legal research and writing.

1980–1987   City of Washington, Department of Finance, Washington, D.C.

Assistant to Financial Analyst

Responsibilities included financial analysis and preparation of financial reports including the annual financial report and financial schedules for bond prospectus.

EXAMPLE: PROBLEM RÉSUMÉ NO. 3

JOHN LEE
3310 15th Street
San Francisco, California 94114
Telephone: (415) 431-1687

PROFESSIONAL OBJECTIVE:	An entry level position in the field of accounting leading to managerial responsibilities.

EDUCATION:
January, 1993

Master of Science
San Francisco State University   San Francisco, California
Majoring in Accounting.
Program included independent study
of Advanced Accounting Theory,
Financial Statements Analysis. Special
Interest in Tax Law.
42 semester hour program completed.
Q.P.R. 3.0 on 4.0 scale.
Thesis: Impacts of Economic Recovery
Tax of 1981 on Investment.

1989–1991

Stanford University   Palo Alto, California
Completed 60 credits of Business Core
Courses.
Accounting. Q.P.R. 3.0 on 4.0 scale.

1989

Bachelor of Arts
University of San Francisco   San Francisco, California
Majoring in Psychology.

Activities: President of Student Drama Club.
          Successfully produced five plays.

WORK HISTORY SUMMARY:
1987–1992

5-years retail experience . . . Cash responsibilities . . .
Assisted management in shipping.
Self-funded 100% of education.

PERSONAL: Determined, strong willed, hard-working, single. Excellent health,
Permanent Legal resident.

REFERENCES: Available upon request.

Problem Résumé 1 has several major problems in layout. First, *the order of items is confusing.* There are two jobs listed, then an educational degree, followed by a third job, and another degree. Although you do want to follow a chronological order, the order should be within major categories, such as Education and Job Experience.

A second problem is related to the first. *There are no section headings to help the reader through the flow of information.*

Margins are a third problem. While you do want to allow sufficient white space to create an open look, this résumé has too much of a good thing.

Finally, looking beyond the layout at the words, *notice the absence of an action-oriented description of job duties and accomplishments.* A reader gets the feeling that the wide margins are there to make up for an absence of content. The résumé looks very formal at first glance, but it is hard to follow, and gives little information.

The major problem with Problem Résumé 2 is the poor judgment in *order.* While there are neat headings and the résumé is easy to read, the information least relevant to the job appears first. Put yourself in the place of the résumé reader. The reader is looking for someone to fill a specific job. Unless that reader is looking for a model or a bouncer, physical qualifications are least important, yet that information comes first. A second problem is the *excessive space given to the bare bones information under education.* The numerous lines of information could be reduced to three or four by using a different format: "J.D., Pace University School of Law, 1988." It is not necessary to give the location of a college unless it would be generally unknown. Because so much space is given to meaningless educational detail, the two honors received are just about lost by the reader. These should be in a special section headed *Honors,* placed between *Education* and *Professional Qualifications.*

Notice how the layout of Problem Résumé 3 calls most attention to the *location* of activities, rather than the *accomplishments* themselves. Notice also how breaking up lines incorrectly makes it almost impossible to figure out what the writer is trying to say, unless you pay close attention and give the résumé a lot of time. No personnel officer reading dozens of résumés will do that. As to content, this résumé is an example of a poor use of the job objective. It should simply have been left out.

Remember that the layout of your résumé should accomplish three important things. It should be clearly organized, so the reader can see quickly what is included. It should emphasize what is most important. It should be neat and attractive to look at, without drawing attention away from the information.

Layout for Your Own Résumé

Take the draft of your résumé and work on a layout. Check the arrangement to see that the areas you think will be most important to the reader appear early in the résumé. If the résumé is getting too cluttered, try to eliminate some of the optional areas, or try to reduce the detail in your earliest job descriptions. You will probably have to try several layouts before you are pleased with the results. You may want to have a friend read over the résumé for clarity of presentation and balance.

Ask your friend to tell you what impresses her or him as most important. Make sure that this is the information that you want to emphasize. If it isn't, make changes to correct it.

Be sure that you use most of the space for the most important information. Allow space between each block of information so each one is easy to spot on the page.

Production and Reproduction

A résumé should be typed on good quality bond paper, either white or ivory. If a word processor is available, you may certainly use it, but there is no need to do so if you have access to a typewriter that produces good, clean copy. All of the employers that we interviewed said that they were not impressed by professionally designed résumé layouts. In fact, several of our experts made the point that they *preferred a straightforward standardized résumé without any special typographical effects.* They felt that overdone résumés indicated that the applicant had been "packaged," and was not presenting facts about herself or himself so much as presenting a fancy image.

After the résumé has been typed, and you have carefully proofread it, you may want to have it commercially reproduced. Quality reproduction does count. You do not want to have a carefully written, organized, and typed résumé marred with copy machine smudges. If you reproduce it yourself, be sure you use a clean machine and the same quality paper on which the original was typed. If you have it done by a copy service, be sure the person understands what you want. Ask for a sample of paper and reproduction quality before you place your order.

One question that often comes up is whether or not you should use any special calligraphy or designs to draw attention to your résumé. The experts' answer to this question was unanimous. Unique typing and layout should be used only when the applicant is applying for a job in which design ability or artistic qualities are important. Then the résumé often serves as an example of the person's work. If you are an applicant for a job in the advertising or printing industries and you would like to use your résumé in this way, take care to keep it appropriate. It is better to be understated in your effects than to have a résumé which produces a laugh! A comment about special designs and art work on the résumé from a personnel director in the advertising field was, "It is so rarely done well. It usually is a turn-off." This is ample warning that getting too fancy with special designs can do more harm than good, unless your job field is art or design and you are an experienced professional. The typefaces you select should add to the overall effect of clarity, directness, and order.

Proofreading

All of the hard work you have done to produce your résumé will have been for nothing if the finished product contains typing or spelling errors. Whether you made the mistake, or the typist did, is unimportant. When you send out the résumé, the error is yours. In this section of the chapter, some basic rules of capitalization and punctuation are given. We have also included three sample résumés which contain errors. Read them carefully to find and correct the errors as practice for proofreading your own résumé.

Rules of Capitalization:

- Capitalize proper nouns such as names of schools, colleges and universities, names of companies, and brand names of products.

- Capitalize major words in the names and titles of books, tests, and articles, in the body of your résumé.

- Capitalize words in major section headings of your résumé.

- Do not capitalize words just because they seem important.

- When in doubt, consult a manual of style such as *Words into Type*, Appleton-Century-Crofts; or *The Chicago Manual of Style*, The University of Chicago Press. Your local librarian can help you locate these and others.

EXAMPLE: PROOFREADING RÉSUMÉ NO. 1

EUGENE HARRIS
_____

2900 Greynolds Street   Deltona, Florida 32725
Home (813)288-4625   Office (305)962-4508

CONTROLLER

Results-oriented financial manager. Proficient in financial analysis, standard costs, job order costs, budgeting, inventory/cost controls and EDP conversions. Experienced with pension programs, insurance, credit and collectionsa nd bank relations.

ACHEIVEMENTS

- Developed and installed financial structure and controls of a new company which facilitated the sale of the business at a substantial profit within six years.

- Directed the design and installation of a computerized financial reporting system for a growth company without no increase in personnel.

- Supervised the design and installation of a tied-in standard cost system which identified scrap and labor variances, thereby saving $200,000.00.

- Strengthened ivnentory controls, which resulted in a $260,000.00 decrease in inventory and minimal inventory adjustments.

- Decreased accounting staff 20% by converting manual posting to computerized job order system.

- Originated a "sound alarm bulletin which tracked percentage-of-completion of jobs, thereby controlling costs.

- Reduced auditing fees 15% by initiating a procedure for preparation of supportion schedules for year-end working papers

- Initiated and installed financial procedures for a highly profitable turnaround situation.

AFFILIATIONS

Amalgamated Systems Inc.	Finance Director
Charles T. Murrow, Inc.	Controller
The Morris Company	Controller/Treasurer
Adams Cable, Inc.	Controller
CPA firms	Staff Acountant

EDUCATION

Baruch College of City University	BBA Accounting
Pace Univ.	Computer Studies

Rules of Punctuation:

- Use a comma to separate words in a series.

- Use a semicolon to separate series of words which already include commas within the series.

- Use a semicolon to separate independent clauses which are not joined by a conjunction.

- Use a period to end a sentence.

- Use a colon to show that the examples or details which follow will expand or amplify the preceding phrase.

- Avoid the use of dashes.

- Avoid the use of brackets.

- If you use any punctuation in an unusual way in your résumé, be consistent in its use.

- Whenever you are uncertain, consult a style manual.

Proofreading Résumé No. 1

The following is a list of errors in the résumé of Eugene Harris:

1. There are no dates given for any jobs.

2. The words *collections and* are mistyped in the first paragraph.

3. *Achievements* is misspelled.

4. The double negative *without no* should be *with no* or *without any*. This kind of error occurs as the writer changes her or his mind as to how to express a thought, but does not change the typing.

5. *Inventory* is misspelled.

6. The closing quotation marks are missing after *alarm*.

7. The writer meant to write *supporting*, not *supportion*.

8. The period at the end of the sentence is missing.

9. A *c* is missing in *accountant*.

10. *University* is unnecessarily abbreviated. This is inconsistent with the other use of the word.

Now try your hand, and eyes, at proofreading the second résumé. Remember, it may have more than simple typographical errors. Circle each error that you find, and check your proofreading against the list provided after the résumé. If you find omissions, write in what you think is missing.

EXAMPLE: PROOFREADING RÉSUMÉ NO. 2

BONNIE THORNTON
236 Bainbridge Street
Malden, Mass. 02148

EXPERIENCE:

Samuel Gompers Co. CPA's (Boston, Mass.)	November, 1985 to Present

Responsible for the palnning and execution of certified and interim audits of diversified client companies. Duties include preparation of time budgets and audit programs review and evaluation of internal accounting controls preparation and analysis of financial statements, and supervised and evaluation of a number of professionals assigned to each audit.

Other responsibilities include the preparation and Review of corporate and partnership income tax returns.

Industries audited include manufacturing, importing, and real estate.

Lewis, Murrow & Company, CPA's (Boston, Mass.)	June, 1976 to November, 1981

Initially with this firm as Semi-Senior Accountant, advancing to senoirity in 1978. Participates in audits of initially smaller client companies and ultimately advanced to auditing responsibilities with larger accounts.

S.J. Tilden & Company, CPA's (Boston, Mass.)	February, 1974 to June, 1977

Gaining my initial experience in the field of public accounting with this frim.

EDUCATION:

Boston College—Graduated in February, with the degree of Bachelor of Science in Accounting. Earned CPA Certificate in August, 1976.

PERSONAL DATA:

Date of Birth: February 12, 1994
Single
Health: Excellent
Affiliations: American Institute of Certified Public Accountants
                N.Y. State Society of Certified Public Accountants

Proofreading Résumé 2   These are the errors you should have found in the résumé of Bonnie Thornton.

1. There is no telephone number by which to reach the applicant.

2. *Planning* is misspelled.

3. Commas are missing in the sentence *Duties include . . . audit.*

4. The word *supervised* should be *supervision* to conform to the rest of the sentence.

5. The word *review* should not be capitalized.

6. *Seniority* is misspelled.

7. *Participates* should be in the past tense, and should be written: *participated*.

8. *Gaining* should also be in the past tense, *gained*.

9. *Public* and *firm* are misspelled.

10. Look at the date of birth. Listing the wrong year is a common error.

Now you are reading for your final test. Proofread Résumé 3 on the next page carefully. Try to find all ten errors before referring to the list below.

Proofreading Résumé 3   The following are the errors you should have found in Martha Stanton's résumé:

1. No address or telephone number is given.

2. Part of the word *objective* is missing.

3. The end of the verb *prepared* is missing. This creates a lack of parallel structure.

4. The words *tax returns* are run together.

5. The word *consulted* is spaced incorrectly.

6. The word *advisory* is misspelled.

7. The job title for the second job is not underlined although the others are.

8. Commas are missing in a series. It should read . . . *rentals, retail-wholesale sales, personal services.*

9. The layout of the first two job descriptions is inconsistent and peculiar.

10. One of the paragraphs of the job descriptions begins with a meaningless *and*.

A Final Suggestion on Proofreading

Proofreading requires a complex combination of skills. Not only do you need to know the rules of punctuation, you need to be able to see small errors in details. If you missed many of the errors in the last practice, it is strongly suggested that you have your résumé proofread by one or more other people before you reproduce or mail out the final copy. The one person probably least able to proofread the résumé is the typist, whether that is you, a devoted friend, or a professional. It is most difficult to see errors after you have typed a piece of work.

If you have now proofread your résumé, the last task is—to proofread it once again. Be sure your résumé represents the best piece of work you can do.

EXAMPLE: PROOFREADING RÉSUMÉ NO. 3

MARTHA STANTON

PROFESSIONAL OBJECT	To join small to medium sized public accounting firm with a near term goal of partnership admission.
WORK EXPERIENCE	A.J. Jackson, C.P.A., Lincoln, Nebraska. <u>Senior Accountant</u>. Responsible for various audit engagements, some of which follow: real estate construction-management-rentals, retail-wholesale sales.
August 1988 to present	• Prepared financial statements with all required generally accepted accounting principle (GAAP) disclosures • Prepare corporation and partnership taxreturns • Consul ted in accordance with management adsivouy standards
February 1986 to August 1988	E.D. Hills & Co., P.A., Lincoln, Nebraska. Senior Accountant. Responsible for various audit engagements, some of which follows: real estate construction-management-rentals retail-wholesale sales personal services limousine services, restaurants, and employment agencies. And assisted managers in other various audit engagements, some of which follow: cable television, construction-management-consulting, retail-wholesale auto parts sales, pension-welfare funds. • Prepared financial statements with all required GAAP disclosures • Prepared corporation-partnership-individual tax returns including pension plan, payroll, and miscellaneous tax returns • Consulting in accordance with management advisory standards
January 1984 to January 1986	LaGuardia & Co. C.P.A.'s, Lincoln, Nebraska. <u>Junior Accountant</u>. Assisted in various audit engagements, some of which follow: manufacturing-sales of yogurt, real estate management-rentals, retail-wholesale sales, personal services.
EDUCATION September 1978	University of Nebraska, Lincoln, Nebraska—B.S. in Accounting Activities included: Accounting and Business Club President, Student-Faculty Academic Standing Committee Board Member, Interdormitory Council Board Member, Dormitory Treasurer and Social Chairman.
MINIMUM SALARY	$25,000
REFERENCES	Furnished upon request

Summary Worksheet

The purpose of this chapter has been to help you present your résumé in the most attractive manner.

Use the list below to check on the appearance of your résumé.

_____ The résumé is centered on the page, with at least one inch margin all around.

_____ There is adequate space between lines and between sections.

_____ Each section is separated from the section before it with a heading such as "Education" or "Work Experience."

_____ All dates are correct.

_____ All names are spelled correctly.

_____ There are no typographical errors.

_____ Experiences are written in action terms.

_____ The reproduced copy is clean.

_____ The reproduced copy is on good bond paper, and not onion skin.

_____ I like the way my résumé looks.

Remember:

There is no one style or paper that is preferable. What is important is neatness, order, and clarity.

Made to order

> *If you are a beginning worker, keep your résumé brief and factual.*

In this chapter, you will see how to tailor your résumé to fit special situations. Four types of special needs are addressed. If you are *looking for your first job*, the first section of this chapter will be helpful. If you are *entering or re-entering the work force* after having been away for a time, the second section is designed for you. If you are *trying to change job fields*, take a look at the third section. If you are looking for work as a consultant, the fourth section is for you. If you have some special needs which you feel cannot be met by using the standard résumé formats suggested in the earlier chapters, the principles presented in the three sections of this chapter will prove helpful.

A: *The New Worker* One strong, common thread ran through the recommendations that employers had for people who are applying for their first jobs—keep the résumé concise, keep it simple, keep it factual, keep it brief. Personnel directors and others who do the hiring like to see that the applicant has put serious, effective effort into preparing the résumé, and a brief, well-written résumé takes time to prepare.

At this point, you may very well be thinking, "But, what should I include?" The following items are the most important, and should be considered first. Then, if you have space, you can add other items.

Education—use the same information and format as suggested for the traditional résumé. Don't try to take up room on your paper by spreading out the items. It should not take four lines to list the diploma or degree you earned, the name of your school, and the dates that you attended there.

Relevant and extraordinary coursework, papers or projects—notice the two key words *relevant* and *extraordinary*. Remember most of the other people who work in the field you hope to enter have had the same basic training or education as you. It is expected that you will have taken the traditional courses for the field. Try to look with some perspective on what you did. Ask yourself, ignoring how hard you may have worked, whether what you did was truly out of the ordinary for someone in your field of study and whether what you did relates to the field that you hope to enter.

Extracurricular activities—there are two main reasons to include these. The first is *to show the breadth and depth of your interest*. List only those activities in which you actively participated. Remember, the person interviewing you may have an interest in the activity you list. The second reason to include these is *to show energy and leadership*. It is important therefore to show any offices you held and your accomplishments within the organization. Remember, however, to keep it brief. The cruel hard fact of the work world is that extracurricular activities are still not considered work. At best, they merely indicate additional skills, interests, and qualities which *might* affect work performance later on.

Work experience—it is likely that you have had some work experience that is completely unrelated to the job you are seeking. Perhaps you worked as a waiter, a library clerk, a dishwasher, or camp counselor. Include these to show that you have been serious about earning a living. Do not try to write the experience so that it looks like more than it was. Remember, most people had the same kinds of jobs when they were starting out. The person who will interview you for the job knows that being a cashier in a cafeteria is only very remotely related to a secretarial career, or accounting, engineering, or computer programming. Just list the job, with a simple one line explanation if that is necessary. If you supported yourself through school, that is an accomplishment to note.

Honors—be sure to note any scholarships you won, distinctions you were awarded for academic excellence, and memberships in honorary organizations. If you made the Dean's List, give dates. If you had excellent grades throughout school in your major, or in your last two years, this may be noted in the beginning where you list your degree.

All of the information tips discussed above related to the information you recorded in your Building Blocks. Turn back to Chapter 1 and look over that information. Review the general suggestions in Chapter 2 on the use of action words, in Chapter 3 on assembling your résumé, and in Chapter 4 on layout and preparation. Finally, use the sample résumés given in the following pages to help you prepare a winning résumé.

EXAMPLE: BEGINNING WORKER'S RÉSUMÉ NO. 1

JUAN C. GARCIA
2103 AFTON STREET
TEMPLE HILL, MARYLAND 20748
HOME (301) 568-2419

EDUCATION:	Columbia University, New York, New York Majors: Politics, Philosophy Degree expected: Bachelor of Arts, 1995 Grade point average: 3.0 Regents Scholarship recipient Columbia University Scholarship recipient
EXPERIENCE:	
7/93–9/93	Graduate Business Library, Columbia University, New York General library duties, entered new students and books onto computer files, gave out microfiche, and reserved materials.
9/92–5/93	German Department, Columbia University, New York Performed general office duties. Provided extensive information assistance by phone and in person. Collated and proofread. Assisted professors gather class material.
6/92–9/92	Loan Collections Department, Columbia University, New York Initiated new filing system in this office. Checked arrears in Bursars Department during registration period.
9/91–6/92	School of Continuing Education, Columbia University, New York. Involved in heavy public contact as well as general clerical duties.
SPECIAL ABILITIES:	Total fluency in Spanish, studying German. Can program in BASIC. Excellent research abilities.
INTERESTS:	Reading, classical music, and foreign travel.
REFERENCES:	Available on request.

EXAMPLE: BEGINNING WORKER'S RÉSUMÉ NO. 2

CAROL A. BADEN

Permanent Address: Temporary Address:
South East Hollow Road   150 Fort Washington Avenue
Berlin, NY 10951   New York, NY 10032
(518) 562-5067   (212) 738-2498

EDUCATION:

Bachelor of Science, Accounting
New York University, New York, N.Y.
Date of Graduation—May 1993
Accounting G.P.A. 3.45
Academic G.P.A. 3.07

PROFESSIONAL
EXPERIENCE:

V.I.T.A. (Volunteer Income Tax Assistance), Spring 1993
Provided income tax assistance to lower income and elderly taxpayers who were unable to prepare returns or pay for professional assistance.

Tutor, Self-employed, September 1990–Present
Helped students to better understand the basic concepts and ideas of accounting.

JOB
EXPERIENCE:

Cook, Summer 1990
Prepared and cooked assorted seafood dishes. I was accountable for deliveries and receiving. (Financed 20% of education.)

General Laborer and Driver, Summers 1988–90
Operated heavy machinery and was involved in other aspects such as delivering materials to and from various job sites. (Financed 50% of education.)

ACTIVITIES
AND
HONORS:

Beta Alpha Psi (Honor Accounting Fraternity), Member
Dean's List Fall 1992 and Spring 1993
A.I.S.E.C.—Association for International Business
Special interest in racquetball and tennis.

EXAMPLE: BEGINNING WORKER'S RÉSUMÉ NO. 3

Ruth M. David
572 First Street
Brooklyn, NY 11215
(212) 789-4328

Education:	New York Law School, New York, New York
	J.D. Candidate, May, 1994
	    Class Rank: Top Twenty-five Percent
	    Student Bar Association Senator, Budget Commission Member
	
	    Associate Editor, Human Rights Journal
	
	University of Wisconsin, Madison, Wisconsin
	B.A. in Political Science, May, 1991
	    Dean's List
	    Marching Band Drill Instructor, Section Leader
	    Residence Hall Council President

Legal Experience:

January, 1993 to May, 1993	Legal Intern Legal Services, Inc., New York, N.Y. Coordinated rehabilitation services provided to mentally handicapped clients at the Mansfield Training School in accordance with federal and state statutes. Analyzed and documented medical and behavioral data of clients in order to revise clients' individual program plans. Monitored institutional procedures to insure statutory compliance, and assisted in research for class action litigation.

Other Experience:

Summer, 1992	Field Manager Citizen Action Group, New York, NY Promoted citizen awareness of state legislative process and issues of toxic waste, utility control, and consumer legislation. Demonstrated effective fund raising and communication methods to the canvass employees. Responsible for developing and sustaining employee motivation and productivity.
August, 1989 to May, 1991	Resident Assistant University of Wisconsin, Office of Residential Life Administered all aspects of student affairs in university residence halls, including program planning, discipline, and individual/group counseling. Directed achievement of student goals through guidance of the residence hall council. Developed and implemented university policies.
August, 1990 to November, 1991	Staff Training Lecturer University of Wisconsin Conducted workshops for residence hall staff on counseling and effective communication. References: Available upon request.

B. The Re-Entering Worker

Use a functional ré-
sumé to stress the
kinds of experience
you have had.

All of the résumés discussed thus far have been in the traditional, *chronological* style. That is, all work experiences
are presented in the order in which schools were attended,
or jobs were held, with the most recent listed first. This is,
in general, the style which personnel officers prefer because it is the style most frequently used and it makes it
easy to compare one résumé to another. However, this type
of presentation may not be the most advantageous to you
in presenting your skills and accomplishments. For the re-
entering worker, the *functional résumé* may work best. It
draws more attention to your skills, and less to the sequence of your work history.

In the functional résumé, your experiences are summed
up by the accomplishments you have had and the skills
you have demonstrated. If you have been a homemaker for
several years, perhaps most of your work outside the home
has been for volunteer organizations, community groups,
or in a variety of seemingly unrelated areas. In this in-
stance, or in other similar ones, the *functional résumé may
be the best approach to use.*

To produce a functional résumé, you need two types of
information. First, you need a strong sense of your own accomplishments and skills. Careful and thorough comple-
tion of all the *Building Blocks* and the *Skills Assessment
Questionnaire* in Chapter 1 is essential. Second, you need a
list of the duties and skills required by the job that you
hope to get, or the field in which you hope to succeed. You
can use the Skills Assessments Questionnaire in Chapter 1
to identify certain jobs. In addition, Appendix C in this
book lists the responsibilities, skills and aptitudes required
for more than 100 jobs.

Keeping your Building Block information and the job
description in mind, re-read the section in Chapter 2 on
writing job-related descriptions. Begin to construct your résumé, not by job title or date, but by *skill area*. All of the
instructions given previously on the sections of the résumé, on layout, and on production still apply. However,
the work experience section will look completely different.

The next sample résumé was prepared by a woman who
worked for several years as a speech teacher and then
stayed home to raise her children. In the time that she was
unemployed (that is, not working for money!), she carried
out several notable civic and community activities. One of
these even took her to Moscow as a representative of the
United States in her special area of interest. When she was
ready to return to work as a full-time employee, she decided she no longer wanted to teach. After some self-
examination, she decided she wanted to enter the com-

puter field. Applying for jobs with her chronological résumé got her nowhere. All of her accomplishments were dismissed as "just volunteer work," or "just teaching." The following résumé got her a job as a systems analyst trainee with a major corporation. This résumé emphasizes the applicant's skills and continuity of interest in a highly specialized language—and this skill related directly to computers and how they are used. As a project director, today she often hires programmers and computer consultants.

EXAMPLE: RE-ENTERING WORKER RÉSUMÉ

Tracy Brinkman
3416 East 57 Street
Cleveland, Ohio 44104
216-387-1384

Objective

Data Processing Trainee.

Work Experience

Abstract Language Use

—formulated rules and wrote teaching manual for mathematical Braille.
—solved unusual problems in code use for Braille transcribers in metropolitan area.
    For the Braille Authority, the Library of Congress and the National Braille Association.

Administrative

—supervised training and maintenance of Braille skills of 20–30 transcribers.
—represented United States at Braille conference in Moscow.
—initiated, organized, and supervised fabrication of 15-foot tapestry by over 300 people.
    For the Industrial Home for the Blind, the World Council for the Welfare of the Blind and Temple Beth Israel, Cleveland.

Teaching

—taught speech to foreign-speaking students.
—taught public speaking.
—taught use of Braille to blind children.
    At Theodore Roosevelt High School, Cleveland.

Education

M.S.—Ohio State University—1984
B.S. *cum laude*—Adelphi College—1982

C. Changing Occupational Directions

If you are in the process of changing occupational directions, there are several techniques you can use to customize your résumé. In the previous section, some tips were given for a re-entering homemaker. That is really a specialized form of career change, and many of the pointers given for that résumé will also apply. You will also need to use the detailed information from your Building Blocks and your knowledge of the qualifications for the new job that you are seeking.

There are three different techniques you can use to tailor your résumé to a change in career:

1. You can use the usual chronological format, *rewriting the description of your accomplishments in terms of the new job or jobs you are seeking.*

2. You can use the chronological résumé, but you *omit experience that is not relevant to the new job.*

3. You can use the *functional*, rather than the chronological format.

The chronological format is the most useful to the interviewer, since the information is in the expected order. You can list your educational, job, and other background in chronological order and simply omit references to work history which will not contribute to your new job goal. Or, you can list those items very briefly, so they do not take attention away from your relevant experience.

The following sample paragraphs were prepared by a job applicant who has held a job managing an information system and computer center at an educational headquarters in a large city. The first description was used to seek a higher position in educational administration. The second description was used to seek a job in the computer industry. Notice the way the same duties are described in different vocabulary and how each sample emphasizes different portions of the applicant's background.

EXAMPLE

For a higher job in educational administration:

Designed and implemented all aspects of new York City's computerized career and college information system including: development of innovative materials for students, counselors, administrators; supervision of program implementation in more than 50 schools; establishing liaison with central office and school personnel; training of counselors and teachers in seminars and on-site; development of evaluation.

EXAMPLE

For a job in the computer industry:

Designed and implemented all aspects of pilot and continuing phases of computerized information system including: assessment of needs; assessment of costs and benefits of various software and hardware options; cyclical review of all files; technical assistance and training to sites; preparation of varying levels of user materials; integration of system into multiple sites; decisions regarding software adaptation and additions; evaluation.

Example—Career Direction Change Résumé No. 1

The first sample résumé was used by an applicant who made the switch from teacher to lawyer. Notice in her résumé, all of her experience as a teacher is omitted, which creates a time gap of about twelve years. She said that she did not receive many questions on the gap in her life as presented on the résumé. In this case, it did little harm to the effect of the résumé, and there was no need to try to explain the abrupt shift in careers.

Example—Career Direction Change Résumé No. 2

The next sample résumé belongs to a man who used it to move from teaching and counseling to personnel work in a corporation. This is in the *functional résumé* style, with a brief chronology of work given later in the résumé. In general, it is more important for a man to account for all his work life on a résumé, than it is for a woman. It is still the expectation of many people that a woman may not work for an employer for long periods of time while she cares for a home or raises children. A gap in employment is, therefore, often less questioned in a woman's résumé than in a man's.

Remember in tailoring your résumé, you can and should produce more than one version. If you are looking at a variety of different jobs, résumés should be written for each one. The purpose is to use the vocabulary that the reader will recognize as appropriate to her or his field, and to stress the accomplishments that you have had that most closely relate to that field.

EXAMPLE: CAREER DIRECTION CHANGE RÉSUMÉ NO. 1

SUSAN GRADY
175 West 68th Street
New York, N.Y. 10023

(work)-(212) 875-5926   (home)-(212) 794-4302

LEGAL EXPERIENCE:
Leonard, Adams & Haber   9/93–present
400 Madison Avenue
New York, NY 10021

Associate. Assist partners in major casualty defense litigation, including medical
malpractice and products liability. Independently handle own case load in all areas
of defense and some plaintiff's litigation. Experience in motion practice, examinations before trial, pre-trial conferences, malpractice panels, jury trials, and appeals.
Substantial client contact, reporting on liability, damages and reserves. Other areas
of practice include corporate, contracts, carriers, property, matrimonial, real estate.

Green & Block   Summer 1992
532 Lexington Avenue
New York, NY 10036

Summer associate.

DISTRICT ATTORNEY, NEW YORK COUNTY   9/91–6/92
1 Hogan Pl.
New York, NY 10013

Clinical associate.

EDUCATION:
BROOKLYN LAW SCHOOL, J.D., 1992
Awards: Dean's List, 1991–92, 1992–93 (TOP TEN PERCENT)
         American Jurisprudence Award—Labor Law I
         American Jurisprudence Award—Evidence II
Honors: Brooklyn Journal of International Law
         Associate Editor, 1992–93
Publications: Torture as a Violation of the Law of Nations:
               Interpreting the Alien Tort Statute,
               7 BROOKLYN J. INT'L. 413 (1992)

UNIVERSITY OF WISCONSIN, B.A., 1978

COLUMBIA UNIVERSITY, TEACHERS COLLEGE, M.A., 1985

BAR ADMISSIONS:
NEW YORK STATE, admitted 2/94
UNITED STATES DISTRICT COURT, SOUTHERN DISTRICT, NEW YORK
UNITED STATES DISTRICT COURT, EASTERN DISTRICT, NEW YORK
FLORIDA, admitted 6/94

EXAMPLE: CAREER DIRECTION CHANGE RÉSUMÉ NO. 2

Gerald Holsten
1205 Maple Avenue
Elsmere, Delaware 19807
Tel. 302-456-7112

Objective: Management position in personnel training and development.

Administration-
Development

Developed intra-school program to improve staff morale and in-struction. Created a special program for incoming high-school stu-dents to facilitate their adjustment to a new environment. Adminis-tered a remediation and orientation program for newly admitted students to high school. Developed and supervised the operations of a college counseling office designed to service 2000 high school students. Planned career and college fair programs for students. School liaison to college admissions and financial aid offices and personnel. Published college and career newsletters.

Counseling-
Placement

Counseled unemployed clients in a training program for the pur-pose of job placement. Provided supportive counseling services to clients while they trained for employment. Vocational, career, college and financial aid counseling and placement for population seeking post-secondary education and training. Individual and group counseling and large group presentations.

Teaching-
Training

Conducted sessions to improve client's communications and job interviewing skills. Trained professional and volunteer staff in col-lege admissions and financial aid counseling. Supervised student-teachers in their training. Taught and developed curricula in psychology, sociology and basic learning skills.

Employment History

1986–Present	—Abraham Lincoln H.S.
1992 (Summer employment)	—GE Employment and Training Systems
1980–1985	—Thomas Jefferson H.S.

Education

B.A. (History), 1980—University of Wisconsin
M.S. (Counseling), 1985 and Advanced Certificate (Counseling), 1986—University of Wisconsin

Affiliations

American Personnel and Guidance Association
American Psychological Association
Association of Teachers of Social Studies

D. Consulting

A functional résumé will often work best to help you in your search for consulting work. That is because you are not expected to present your entire work history, only that which pertains to the work you are seeking.

Often in consulting, you are recommended for a position and even have an interview before your résumé is seen. Nevertheless, particularly in a large organization, someone will want your résumé sooner or later to "prove" that you have the background necessary to complete the work successfully, as a record of what you discussed, or to share with a colleague or partner in making the decision.

Experienced consultants may have pages and pages of related work to report. Just as with résumés for other purposes, it is important that all the experience be distilled to its essence, and that the essence take no more than two pages. The sample consultant's resume shows how to present a lot of information in under two pages. Notice in the résumé as well that some information is provided for the major accomplishments, but the usual requirements of dates and names of organizations may be handled with less detail. Of course, you may be asked to provide references so all that you present should be verifiable.

EXAMPLE: CONSULTANT'S RÉSUMÉ

Boris Stanton
4321 Hibiscus Way
Miami, FL 33009
(305) 475-6903

SUMMARY
- Systems professional with over 20 years experience as a Programmer, Systems Analyst, Consultant, Manager, Group Leader, and EDP Instructor. Considerable background in FORTRAN, COBOL, Basic on mainframes, minis, and micros in a wide variety of technical and general business application. Holder of BS in Physics, MS in Math, and MBA in Statistics and Computer Methodology. Experienced, comfortable, and proficient in leading large and small sessions.

MAJOR ACCOMPLISHMENTS
- Chosen by consortium of physicians and dentists to evaluate current micro systems available for office automation and accounting applications. The hardware investigated included IBM PC, Apple, Toshiba, and DEC. The software investigated included Software Hows, SYcom, Univar and Micro Soft.

- For First National Bank of Florida wrote a system to allocate funds to 700 support centers. The application involved over 20 major sub-systems and programs. The system was written in FORTRAN and COBOL on Prime mini and used OR techniques such as Linear Programming.

- At American Limited designed, implemented, and installed a Bond Trading System. The system produced daily reports that enabled traders to have accurate, timely information of client positions. The system was written in RAMIS under TSO/SPF.

- Instructor at University of Miami, teaching advanced computer science courses, both on graduate and undergraduate levels. Courses taught include: Advanced FORTRAN, Advanced COBOL, Statistical Methods, and Operations Research.

- At College of Insurance—led seminars in Systems Analysis for insurance executives.

EMPLOYMENT HISTORY

1973–Present   Independent consultant involved in providing processing services to a wide variety of clients and Instructor at University of Miami, Department of Statistics and Computer Information Systems.

1970–1973   Programmer for ITT and Computer Usage Company. Programmed in FORTRAN, COBOL, and Assembler on IBM equipment.

EDUCATION

City University of New York, MBA, Computer Methodology, 1980

Yeshiva University, MS, Mathematics, 1972

City College of New York, BS, Physics, 1967

Summary Worksheet

The purpose of this chapter was to help you design your résumé for special situations. To do this, you need to do the work recommended in the first three chapters, and then rearrange and rewrite your résumé to fit the situation. Then you must return to Chapter 4 to be sure your résumé looks good.

Use this checklist to review the steps you followed.

_____ I reviewed my skills and accomplishments in Chapter 1, "Building Blocks."

_____ I rewrote my experiences and activities using action words and job descriptions.

_____ I read about the essential and optional parts of a résumé in Chapter 3.

_____ I reviewed the descriptions of jobs that interest me in Appendix C.

_____ I selected my skills, accomplishments, experiences and activities which are most closely related to the job I am seeking.

_____ I arranged my experiences in a way the reader can understand.

_____ I looked at the sample résumés for ideas.

_____ I rearranged and rewrote my résumé.

_____ I typed, proofread and copied my résumé.

Remember:

Keep the résumé concise, keep it simple, keep it factual, keep it brief.

Distribution

Use the cover letter as an effective introduction to your résumé.

To handle the distribution of your résumé effectively you will need to prepare a cover letter and set up a system of keeping records of résumés you have sent out.

There are generally two ways of distributing your résumé. One is to deliver it in person. Perhaps you have an appointment with a contact who you hope will recommend you for a job. Maybe you are going to see a person to whom you've been recommended. In any of these kinds of situations, you will want to have a copy of your résumé ready to leave with the person.

The more frequently used method of distributing your résumé is to mail it with a letter in response to an advertisement or some other job lead. Whenever you mail your résumé, you must also send a cover letter. This chapter will help you write Winning Cover Letters. Appendices A and B provide information on how to find select people to whom you'll send your résumé and cover letter.

Remember that the cover letter is designed to introduce the résumé and interest your potential employer in reading it, just as the résumé is designed to interest that person in meeting you. The cover letter must be neat and clean both in content and production.

Sections of the Cover Letter

The cover letter should include the following sections:

1. Your address (unless it is typed on your personal letterhead which already includes this information).

2. The date.

3. The address of the person and company to whom you are sending the résumé. If you are addressing a post office box number in an advertisement, include the box number information. Use the salutation, "To whom it may concern:" to open the letter.

4. The first paragraph should explain why you are writing. Is the letter in response to an advertisement, the result of a previous meeting, at the suggestion of a common acquaintance?

5. The next one or two paragraphs should relate one or two highlights of your experience to the job's needs.

6. The final paragraph should close with a request for an interview and any pertinent information needed to schedule it. This might include hours at which you can be reached at a particular telephone number, or days when you will be in the area if the job is not near your home location.

7. Whether the letter is addressed to a classified ad box number or to an individual, the correct closing is, "Sincerely," or "Yours truly," followed by your signature, followed by your full name typed out.

Writing the Cover Letter

A cover letter, including all the information above, should be one page in length. The language should be businesslike and to the point. Avoid overblown language. One cover letter after the standard opening paragraph, included the following:

EXAMPLE—PROBLEM COVER LETTER

I believe that my résumé bespeaks the qualifications necessary to excel at the position. . . . I have a ceaseless capacity to overcome challenges in skills applications.

The example above is much too flowery and misses the point by hiding it in too many words. On the other hand, you can be too brief. The following letter was handwritten on a piece of lined yellow paper torn from a pad, ripped in half at the bottom.

EXAMPLE—PROBLEM COVER LETTER

Dear Sirs:
    Enclosed is my résumé in response to your notice in the NY *Times*. My present salary is at $54,000. I can be contacted during business hours with proper discretion. Thank you for your consideration.
                Sincerely

                Gerald French

Two examples of well-written cover letters appear on subsequent pages. Both were written to the same company, one in response to an advertisement, the other as part of the applicant's campaign to change jobs, moving to a particular type of company.

Producing the Cover Letter

The cover letter should always be an individually typed one-page document on good bond paper. Since the cover letter must be written to particular individuals, or at least to particular companies, they cannot be reproduced or photocopied like résumés. Of course, once you have written and rewritten your first cover letter to the point where you really like it, you can certainly use the same or similar wording in subsequent letters.

    After the cover letter has been typed, be sure to proofread it as carefully as you did the résumé. Handle it carefully to avoid a dirty or smudged appearance. Mail the cover letter and résumé in an envelope of the appropriate size.

Recordkeeping

After the last chapter, you will find a list of detailed resources to help you identify potential recipients of your résumés. Many job hunting manuals emphasize the importance of contacts. While contacts are a valuable resource, many people have found jobs they like through newspaper ads, personnel agencies, and other means. Broadcasting your résumé, that is, sending it unsolicited to *many* companies, is not considered by many job placement experts to be an efficient means of job hunting. Yet, there are people who have gotten jobs they really wanted and liked by mailing résumés to all the companies under appropriate headings in the classified telephone directory.

Résumé Records

Whatever method of distribution you use, it is important that you keep a record of the résumé you have sent and the results. One method is to make photocopies of your cover letters and to note any response and interviews on them. Another method is to use a chart like the ones that follow the sample cover letter. A sample is filled in to illustrate how it is used.

EXAMPLE: COVER LETTER NO. 1

THOMAS E. WESTBRIDGE
ATTORNEY AT LAW
5805 GROVE RIDGE STREET
3RD FLOOR
HOUSTON, TEXAS 77061
(713) 486-4322

June 20, 19____

Dept. 12572
1501 Polk Avenue
Houston, Texas 77002

Dear Sirs:

I have specialized, for the last fifteen years, in tax planning on the federal, international and local levels. I was fortunate to have had broad and intensive experience in most phases of the tax law, representing "big board" and multinational corporations, as well as top-level executives. I worked closely and frequently with "big-eight" accounting firms.

I am currently seeking a position with a "Fortune 500" corporation as tax attorney or with similar duties. I would bring to the position analytical expertise as to existing and future tax strategies, acquisitions and dispositions, and compliance.

My primary objective is to secure a position that offers challenge and opportunity to assume responsibility and exercise independent judgment.

I am available for a conference with you at your convenience. Please call at (212) 486-4322 during the day.

Very truly yours

Thomas E. Westbridge

Thomas E. Westbridge

EXAMPLE: COVER LETTER NO. 2

689 Grant Avenue
Virginia Beach, Virginia 23457
June 21, 19_____

Dept. 12572
1501 Polk Avenue
Houston, Texas 77002

Dear Sir:

Enclosed please find my résumé in response to your recent ad in *The Wall Street Journal* for a tax attorney. I am an attorney, admitted to practice in New York. In addition to being an attorney, I am a certified public accountant. I have a master's degree in accounting and an undergraduate degree in finance.

Prior to attending law school I was employed by Peat, Marwick, Mitchell & Co., a large public accounting firm. While in law school and up to the present time I have been employed by a corporation. My current position entails federal tax research and planning, some compliance work, as well as general legal work and special financial projects.

I am interested in continuing to use my legal and financial experience in an environment which will provide the opportunity for continued professional growth. Therefore, I would like to learn more about the position you have open. I would be happy to arrange an interview, at your convenience, to discuss this matter in greater detail. I can be reached during the day at (804) 912-1300, and in the evening at (804) 315-7582.

Very truly yours

Arthur D. DeMille

Arthur D. DeMille

Example

SENT TO: **Name:** George B. Hayes
Title: Vice President
Company: Sonotext Systems, Inc.
Address: 4044 Garfield Avenue South
City, State, Zip: Minneapolis, Minn. 55409
Telephone: (612) 784-1096
RESULTS: **Date:** 1/11/94, First Interview; 7/28/94 recalled.
Names: Saw Eugene H. Perler; George B. Hayes; Marilyn Mayle. Perler appears to be the decision-maker because it is his department. Place of Mayle in decision is unclear.
Action: Had two interviews; wrote thank you notes; still seems a possible opening.

Résumé Record No. 1

SENT TO: Name _____

Title _____

Company _____

Address _____

City, State, Zip _____

Telephone _____

RESULTS: Date _____

Names _____

_____

Action _____

Résumé Record No. 2

SENT TO: **Name** _____

Title _____

Company _____

Address _____

City, State, Zip _____

Telephone _____

RESULTS: **Date** _____

Names _____

_____

Action _____

Résumé Record No. 3

SENT TO: **Name** _____

Company _____

Address _____

City, State, Zip _____

Telephone _____

RESULTS: **Date** _____

Names _____

_____

Action _____

_____

```
┌─────────────────────────────────────────────────────────┐
│                  Résumé Record No. 4                      │
│                                                           │
│ SENT TO:  Name _____   │
│                                                           │
│           Company _____   │
│                                                           │
│           Address _____   │
│                                                           │
│           City, State, Zip _____   │
│                                                           │
│           Telephone _____   │
│                                                           │
│ RESULTS:  Date _____   │
│                                                           │
│           Names _____   │
│                                                           │
│                 _____   │
│                                                           │
│           Action _____   │
│                                                           │
│                 _____   │
└─────────────────────────────────────────────────────────┘
```

Use as many charts as needed. They can be made up on 5″ × 7″ index cards and filed alphabetically by the name of the addressee or the name of the company. Check your records daily, and keep them up-to-date. If you do not hear from an individual or a company in a reasonable length of time, you can call and ask if the letter and résumé have been received. If not, you can send another one. If they have been received, find out when you can expect a response, if any additional information would be useful, and if there is a set date by which they expect to fill the job.

Summary Worksheet

The purpose of this chapter was to help you prepare to distribute your résumé. To do this, you need to write one or more cover letters. You also need to set up a recordkeeping system so that you know where you've sent your résumé, whom you have seen, and which job leads are still possibilities.

Use this checklist below to review your distribution procedures.

_____ I have written at least one sample cover letter.

_____ I have selected a good bond paper on which to type my letters.

_____ For each résumé I have sent, I have typed a separate cover letter.

_____ I have proofread every letter before it was mailed.

_____ I have prepared a notebook, index cards or a folder in which I keep track of the résumés I have sent or given out.

Remember:

The cover letter is designed to introduce the résumé and interest your potential employer in reading it.

Beauty is in the eye of the beholder

Listen to the experts' advice to make your résumé appeal to the reader.

When you write a résumé, remember that a winning résumé appeals to the reader. This reader, the person who has the power to take you to the next step in your job search, is the reader whose eye you want to catch. Therefore the material in this book is based not only on the author's experience as a career counselor, but on interviews with people responsible for hiring others. The employers, or hiring officials and personnel officers interviewed, were in a variety of industries including accounting, advertising, computers, insurance, law, education, banking, retailing, and health services. They have had responsibility for hiring, at different times in their careers, people at all levels of experience and expertise from beginning workers to the highest level of corporate executives. Although throughout this book they are referred to as personnel or hiring officers, their actual positions in their organizations range from those initially responsible for recruitment to company executives who have the final say on hiring.

The author interviewed these hiring officials, asking each of them a series of carefully planned questions.

The interview had two parts. All of the experts were asked seven general questions about résumés and what they liked, and did not like, to see in them. In addition, they were all asked to comment on the usefulness of specific résumé items, such as "job objective" and "age." Their comments on the résumé sections have already been presented in Chapter 3, "Assembly." What follows in the rest of this chapter are summaries of their answers to the seven key questions with direct quotations from the experts to help you in designing and presenting your winning résumé.

Question 1   What is the first thing you look for when a résumé crosses your desk?

Answers   The most frequently given reply related directly to *relevant work experience.* Some of the items which were mentioned several times were the following:

"Direct experience for the position I am trying to fill."

"A cover letter showing the purpose of the résumé."

"I take a fast glance at a person's education. Then I look for specific experiences, ability, knowledge, skills."

"I look for evidence of initiative, intelligence, and energy running through the résumé."

"I want a short covering letter. I want the résumé on time. If I ask for salary requirement, I want to see it. Otherwise I may be wasting my time, or theirs."

"People in my company need experience on word processors. If it's not there, they are knocked out."

"If it's an entry level job, I look for the school they attended and their grade point average. If it's for an experienced worker, I look for the type of firm they were with, the functions they performed, and the number of jobs they have held."

"The job experience, especially in the last five years."

Question 2   Many people have résumés prepared on word processors, or have them run off in bulk printing. Others type them on ordinary bond paper. What is your preference about how you want the résumé to look?

Answers None of the people interviewed had a preference about whether the résumé was individually typed, photocopied, or printed. They did care whether it was clear and clean. Here are some of their responses:

"I want good, clean copy. I want clarity with headings to organize the material."

"I don't care about paper, but typographical errors are terrible. It shows me the person is careless or lackadaisical. It disturbs me that they would allow this to appear. My business requires attention to detail. If they cannot get their résumé right, can they do the work?"

"I don't want anything far out. I don't want big paragraphs with the history of the person. I like the ordinary style."

"I don't care about the preparation, but I don't want a form letter sent out to everyone."

"The résumé should be one page."

"The quality of the production is what counts. Is it typed straight on the page? Did they use an ugly, dingy, xerox copy? I like a personalized cover letter."

"The production doesn't affect my judgment unless it's really sloppy—done on some crazy copy machine."

"I don't want onion skin."

"Anything over two pages is just packaging. Cut it out."

Question 3 Résumés have many sections—education, work history, professional associations, and so on. Which do you prefer to see first?

Answers All but two of the experts preferred to see *education* first. One of the officers in an accounting firm said that *work history* should be first. However, he also said that he *looks at* education first. A representative of the computer industry said that knowledge of particular machines and languages should come first. Here are some of the specific comments:

"Education shows you a person's formal credentials."

"Although work history is of first importance, education should be at the top in a very brief form."

"The chronology is more orderly with education first. It helps my mind."

"I like to look at the top line to see how far someone has gone in her or his education."

"The way I read résumés is that I put them in a pile. Then I go through the whole pile, just looking at education, and so on. I want to find education in the top third of the first sheet."

Question 4   Some résumés are written in chronological order, others by function. Which of these styles do you prefer?

Answers   *Not only did all of the personnel officers prefer the chronological style, most were not familiar with what was meant by a functional résumé.* The only exception was the woman who had used one herself when she returned to the work force after an absence. Their comments were:

"I expect to see a chronological order. It makes it easier to review."

"The typical person who reviews résumés, reviews many. The best chance to catch attention is to *present concisely*. The chronological order is less cluttered."

"Functional? I wondered where they came from. I prefer the chronological with the most recent first. In the other kind you have to look in several places for work experiences."

"Some people like to use flair. I'm not looking for an artistic flair. I want to find things where I know they are going to be."

The functional résumé is obviously not a favorite.

Question 5   What recommendations as to résumé writing would you make to a young person applying for her or his first job?

Answers   There were two major pieces of advice: the first was to be *as concise as possible*, the second was to be *factual and down-to-earth*. Some specific suggestions were:

"List only real achievements. If you have none, write a sincere cover letter stating your goals and your willingness to work hard."

"Make the résumé fit the job. There is no résumé that will fit every job."

"I like to see how well one got through college—interests, honors, energy."

"Show me how your experience in college fits with the knowledge we need in the company."

"Be as terse as possible. Give details on only the most recent and significant experiences. Try to arouse interest in the reader, so you can flesh out the details in the interview."

"If I get a résumé of more than two pages from a young person, I'm getting fluff."

"Spend a lot of time conveying what it is you want to say so that you can say it as concisely as possible. I like to see evidence that someone has put effort into the communication."

"Let the résumé show me your ability to communicate succinctly in writing."

"Be honest. Be factual. Avoid exaggeration at all costs."

Question 6 What is your policy if you discover that an applicant has falsified her or his background on the résumé?

Answers All of the personnel officers agreed that falsification of any significant data would eliminate the candidate. They said that if a person had minor exaggerations—said they had worked for two years when they had only worked for one year and nine months—this would not necessarily eliminate them. However, they all also indicated that even these minor lies would make them uncomfortable and if they had other qualified applicants, they would rather not select the person who was less than honest. Some of the responses were:

"I try to ignore minor exaggerations, but you cannot make up jobs or degrees—say you were a manager when you were a clerk."

"Throw it in the garbage."

"Integrity is very important. Even a small lie is a minus on integrity. If I hired that person, I would never feel sure."

Your best bet is to be impeccably honest and accurate in stating your experience and accomplishments.

Question 7   We began by talking about the most important thing you look for in a résumé; I'd like to end with what you consider the worst sin, or most unattractive mistake that people frequently make in their résumés. What really turns you off?

Answer   There are *three fatal errors. All* of the people interviewed mentioned *all three*. The first fatal error is *wordiness*. The second fatal error is *sloppiness*. The third fatal error is a *lack of honesty*. Here are the final words of advice on the mistakes that you will want at all costs to avoid:

"Wordiness makes me think a person doesn't have enough experience."

"Using white-out or other obvious techniques to make changes means the person didn't want to go to the effort of preparing a new résumé for my job."

"A lack of parallel structure shows me there was a lack of editing effort. Write, 'I organized,' 'I collected,' 'I assisted,' and so on."

"Don't have spelling errors."

"Don't try to create a false sense of drama and glory. The worst sin is when someone just out of college tries to make a big thing out of a part-time job, and writes 'coordinated sanitary operations' when she kept the key to the ladies' room."

"I don't want to see anything that gives me a credibility problem. Above all, don't lie to me."

"I hate something too overblown, too packaged, with seven or eight pages, and arrangements by both chronology and function. It leads me to question the candidate's sense of herself or himself. My résumé should demonstrate what I'm about and show I have a focused understanding of what I'm going after. Poor wording, sloppiness, typos, wrong names, and titles are terrible in a résumé because a résumé needs to communicate a standard by which you operate."

Final Summary Worksheet   Now your résumé is just about finished. You have written one or several cover letters. You have decided how you want to keep track of distribution.

You want to be sure that all of your hard work will pay off in a winning résumé. This final checklist will help you take one hard, last look at your work.

_____ I have included the essentials—my name, address, telephone numbers.

_____ My education is given completely, but in just a few lines of type.

_____ My work experience gives dates and companies.

_____ I have included other experiences that show my skills, accomplishments and energy.

_____ I know why I have included each piece of information.

_____ My writing uses action words and job-related vocabulary.

_____ I have avoided grand sounding phrases.

_____ I have not puffed up experiences to be more than they were.

_____ I like the way my résumé looks on the page. There are even margins, and spacing helps the reader along.

_____ I have proofread my résumé for spelling and typographical errors.

_____ I have made sure my résumé is copied on good paper.

_____ I have looked at the photocopies to be sure they are clean.

_____ I have included my address and the company address on each cover letter.

_____ Each cover letter tells the job I am applying for, or why I am sending my résumé.

_____ I have proofread my cover letters..

_____ I understand what employers are looking for in a résumé.

_____ I have written a winning résumé.

Appendix A

Sources of Job Leads   Following is a list of resources you can use to locate possible job leads and potential recipients of your résumé.

Newspaper classified advertisements

Business, Education, Health and other special sections of newspapers

Personal contacts through friends and relatives

Contacts made through projects in school

Professional and trade journals and newspapers

Professional association conference placement services (Many provide annual books with listings of résumés and job openings)

College and university placement offices

Professors and teachers (past and present)

Private and State employment service agencies

Federal Job Information Centers

Classified telephone directories (Yellow Pages)

Chamber of Commerce lists

Unions

Appendix B

Additional Sources of Information

There are many directories of business, which are available in business and general libraries. Some of them are:

Dun and Bradstreet's Million Dollar Directory. New York.

Standard & Poor's Register of Corporations, Directors and Executives. New York.

Standard Directory of Advertisers. Skokie, Illinois.

Thomas Register of American Manufacturers and Thomas Register Catalog File. New York.

U.S. Industrial Directory. Denver, Colorado.

American Register of Exporters and Importers. New York.

Directory of Firms Operating in Foreign Countries. New York.

Dun & Bradstreet's Metalworking Directory. New York.

Bottin International: International Business Register. Paris.

Dun & Bradstreet's Principal International Businesses. New York.

Fraser's Canadian Trade Directory. Toronto.

Occupational Outlook Handbook. Washington, D.C. This is not a directory of firms or businesses, but is an excellent resource for job descriptions to help in your résumé writing or career selection. Current information about the numbers of jobs in the fields, sources of information, and related reading are also included.

Appendix C

100-plus Job Descriptions

The following job descriptions can help you prepare your résumé in several ways. First, you can use the job descriptions after you complete the Skills Profile on pages 24 to 26 to see descriptions of jobs that match your skills. Second, you can use the descriptions with the Skills Profile to see what jobs are _similar_ to jobs you have already held. Third, in writing your work experience sections of your résumé, you can review the duties, skills, and aptitudes you have displayed in jobs you have held. Fourth, you can use the language of the job descriptions when you rewrite your experiences for the résumé. Finally, if you are in an early stage of career choice, you can use the job descriptions to help you identify jobs you would like to learn more about.

Accountants and Auditors

Responsibilities: Compile and analyze business records. Prepare financial reports needed for effective management. Devise accounting systems and procedures. Appraise assets and investment programs.

Aptitudes and Skills: Ability to concentrate for long periods; organize work; operate business machines; prepare complete and accurate accounting reports. Memory for detail. Knowledge of accounting principles and methods; data processing techniques. Good vocabulary and communication skills. Speed and accuracy with numbers.

Administrators, Educational

Responsibilities: Manage school systems to promote satisfactory business and academic operations for staff and students. Recruit and hire personnel; prepare and manage budgets. Develop policies and programs. Supervise teaching and non-teaching staff.

Aptitudes and Skills: Ability to analyze problems; organize plans and ideas; make decisions; respond to changing needs; deal with people individually and in groups. Strong communication skills. Knowledge of law, budgets, personnel practices, organizational theory and educational theory.

Administrators, Health Services

Responsibilities: Coordinate hospitals and other health facilities and their staffs to assure satisfactory patient care. Organize personnel. Hire and supervise staff. Maintain good public relations.

Aptitudes and Skills: Ability to relate to people; prepare financial reports; solve complex problems; organize and direct large scale activities; plan and implement policies. Knowledge of financial management; purchasing; fund raising; data processing.

Administrators, Public

Responsibilities: Coordinate and direct public services to meet the needs of the nation, state, or community. Analyze problems; work with special committees and public agencies; recommend solutions to governing bodies.

Aptitudes and Skills: Ability to relate to and communicate with people; solve complex problems through analysis; plan, organize, and implement policies and programs. Knowledge of political systems; financial management; personnel administration; program evaluation; organizational theory.

Agricultural Scientists

Responsibilities: Apply principles of physical and biological sciences to protect, develop and manage agricultural resources. Develop methods of growing crops with higher yield and improved strains. Study the characteristics and behavior of soils. Solve problems such as erosion and loss of moisture. Develop means of preserving and developing natural resources.

Aptitudes and Skills: Ability to work with words and numbers; make decisions; use appropriate tools, aerial photographs, mapmaking and laboratory equipment. Knowledge of scientific theories and data; of physical, earth and biological sciences.

Air Traffic Controllers

Responsibilities: Coordinate the flights of aircraft to prevent accidents and minimize delays in takeoffs and landings. Monitor aircraft; electronic landing and navigational aids; airport lights. Issue clearances; radar vectors; traffic information.

Aptitudes and Skills: Must have good health; vision correctable to 20/20; clear, precise speech. Ability to work under stress; to think abstractly in order to conceptualize the entire air traffic picture; to establish priorities rapidly; to think clearly in emergencies; to have automatic recall; to listen to more than one pilot at one time. Specific knowledge set by the FAA.

Architects

Responsibilities: Design structures and areas to satisfy a client's functional and aesthetic requirements. Draw plans, sketches; specifications. Monitor building construction. Provide information about building costs and materials.

Aptitudes and Skills: Ability to organize; to visualize spatial relationships; to communicate ideas graphically, orally and in writing. Knowledge of planning and designing, drafting, construction methods and materials, business management. Creativity.

Biologists   *Responsibilities:* Teach and study all aspects of living matter including the origin, identification and classification of life processes, behavior, diseases and structure of all life forms. Research such problems as damage and disease caused by insects and animals. Work in laboratories or the field observing animals and plants in their natural habitats.

Aptitudes and Skills: Attention to detail. Very high intellectual and mathematical ability; spatial and form perception. Knowledge of scientific theories; field and laboratory procedures. Very good writing and speaking skills.

Bookkeepers   *Responsibilities:* Record day-to-day business transactions on various accounting forms. Prepare summary statements; customers' bills; data entry forms. Sometimes do other general office tasks such as telephone answering.

Aptitudes and Skills: Ability to work with numbers; to concentrate on details. Knowledge of business arithmetic and bookeeping procedures; of data processing; of business machines. Good eye-hand coordination.

Business Executives   *Responsibilities:* Develop and administer policies to increase profits and make organizations run smoothly. Review and establish goals; coordinate plans; make necessary procedural changes. Direct major programs. Take overall responsibility for all levels of functions within their jurisdictions. Have "bottom-line" responsibility for profits and losses.

Aptitudes and Skills: Ability to communicate with others; to develop long-range goals and objectives; to establish effective communication throughout an organization. Knowledge of problem-solving; decision-making; personnel administration; organizational theory. Leadership.

Buyers

Responsibilities: Purchase goods for their firms to resell. Talk with people; negotiate contracts.

Aptitudes and Skills: Ability to work with people; work on details; communicate orally and in writing; work with numbers. Knowledge of merchandising; purchasing practices; marketing techniques; pricing methods and discounting; inventory control.

Chemists

Responsibilities: Research and teach the composition, structure, synthesis, and reaction of matter. Experiment with various substances; analyze data; test samples.

Aptitudes and Skills: Ability to work independently with thoroughness, attention to detail, patience, and perseverance. High intellectual, verbal, and mathematical ability. Above average spatial and form perception. Knowledge of scientific theory; laboratory techniques; principles of chemistry.

Chiropractors

Responsibilities: Diagnose and treat spinal-related disorders to aid patients in regaining and maintaining good health. Duties may include signing birth and death certificates; performing minor surgery; emphasis is on the function of the nervous system. The primary therapy method is spinal manipulation.

Aptitudes and Skills: Ability to work independently; make decisions. Good hand and finger dexterity. Knowledge of anatomy; chemistry; physiology; microbiology; chiropractic principles; adjustive techniques; x-ray techniques; diagnosis; physiotherapy; office procedures.

Claims Adjustors and Examiners

Responsibilities: Review and process loss or damage claims made against insurance companies. Gather facts by interview; consult police and hospital records; inspect damaged property; analyze claims; determine extent of the company's liability. Prepare reports.

Aptitudes and Skills: Ability to deal with all kinds of people; to make decisions; to assume responsibility. Knowledge of laws and regulations governing the insurance industry. Above average verbal and numerical skills.

Commercial Artists

Responsibilities: Illustrate ideas through sketches, drawings and other works. Prepare artwork for newspapers, magazines, advertisements, book illustrations, designs on commodity packages.

Aptitudes and Skills: Ability to visualize ideas on paper; to design; to prepare mechanicals; to estimate time needed to complete a project; to work under pressure to meet deadlines. Knowledge of tools; layout techniques; composition. Aesthetic appreciation. Visual creativity. Form perception. Color discrimination.

Computer Operators

Responsibilities: Monitor and control computers to process data according to pre-determined instructions. Select and load input and output units with materials such as tapes or printout forms. Observe the machines for stoppage or faulty input.

Aptitudes and Skills: Ability to approach problems meticulously; to follow detailed and organized procedures. Knowledge of computer systems and equipment; of technical language used in operating instructions and computer manuals; typing.

Computer Programmers

Responsibilities: Write computer programs and other coded instructions for computers to perform a desired task. Decide upon the information needed to solve a problem; prepare a flowchart; write complete, step-by-step instructions. Test programs; correct errors. Write documentation.

Aptitudes and Skills: Ability to organize ideas and data; to communicate technical information orally and in writing; to organize time to meet deadlines; to work with little room for error. Knowledge of programming techniques and limitations. Above average numerical ability and clerical perception.

Computer Repairers

Responsibilities: Maintain and repair computers and computer-related equipment. Install equipment. Provide routine service including cleaning and oiling mechanical parts; checking electronic equipment. Determine the cause of breakdowns and replace parts. Answer customers' questions on maintenance.

Aptitudes and Skills: Mechanical, numerical, spatial abilities. Good close vision; normal color perception; normal hearing. Knowledge of electronics; of elementary computer theory, computer math, circuitry theory; of proper use and care of specialized tools and testing equipment; of appropriate technical manuals; of preventive maintenance record-keeping procedures. Ability to deal with people; to work under pressure. Knowledge of programming helpful.

Construction Superintendents

Responsibilities: Plan and direct building projects to satisfy the contractor's specifications and schedules. Coordinate the activities of skilled workers, supervisors and subcontractors. Order tools and materials. Inspect projects and prepare reports on materials used, cost and progress.

Aptitudes and Skills: Ability to interpret instructions in written, oral, diagrammatic or schedule form; to understand drawings and specifications; to do arithmetic quickly and accurately; to estimate costs. Knowledge of construction materials and practices; building codes; contract specifications.

Counselors

Responsibilities: Work in schools and agencies to help others to understand themselves better and to apply that understanding to living and working more effectively. May administer tests; interpret test scores; work with individuals; conduct group sessions; do staff development.

Aptitudes and Skills: Ability to communicate well; to accept responsibility; to select tests; to interpret test scores;

to help others examine their interests, needs and goals. Knowledge of counseling theory; interview techniques; developmental theory; world of work; human behavior. Patience. Concern for human welfare.

Dental Hygienists

Responsibilities: Working under the general supervision of a dentist; help people develop and maintain good oral health. Clean and polish teeth; note conditions of decay and disease; take and develop x-rays. Teach patients proper dental care. May sterilize instruments; keep records.

Aptitudes and Skills: Knowledge of dental hygiene procedures such as fluoride and x-ray treatment. Ability to prepare clinical and laboratory diagnostic tests for the dentist; to communicate on a one-to-one basis with the patient; to pay precise attention to detail. Good manual and finger dexterity; eye-hand coordination; cleanliness; health.

Dentists

Responsibilities: Diagnose and treat patients' teeth to prevent and correct dental problems. Most dentists are in general practice. Some are specialists such as orthodontist, periodontist, prosthodontist.

Aptitudes and Skills: Knowledge of diagnostic techniques and treatment procedures; the use of dental equipment; of scientific principles. Ability to judge space and shape; to work with people; to communicate orally and in writing.

Designers, Clothes

Responsibilities: Design and construct garments using sketches and sample garments. From these, make fullsize paper and/or fiberboard patterns.

Aptitudes and Skills: Ability to sketch ideas on paper; to adapt body measurements to a paper pattern; to sew; to draft patterns; to adjust patterns for fit and appearance; to estimate the cost of making a garment. Knowledge of clothing styles; textiles; fabrics; types of sewing machines; color coordination. Creativity. Finger dexterity.

Designer, Floral   *Responsibilities:* Prepare floral arrangements for a variety of occasions using flowers, greenery and artificial aids. Arrangements must be appropriate for the event and meet customer specifications as to color, flower preference, cost.

Aptitudes and Skills: Ability to work standing for long periods; to lift containers of flowers weighing up to 40 pounds; to work with people. Accurate color vision. Manual dexterity. Artistic ability.

Designers, Interior   *Responsibilities:* Plan interior space to enhance the attractiveness and function of commercial and residential buildings. Consult with clients and architects; select colors, fabrics, floor and wall coverings, light fixtures, cabinetwork, furniture, accessories.

Aptitudes and Skills: Knowledge of colors; textures; principles of design. Ability to work with people; communicate verbally and through sketching. Creativity. Flexibility. Good business judgment.

Dietitians   *Responsibilities:* Plan nutritious meals to help people maintain or recover good health. Plan menus and diets for therapeutic treatment; plan menus and supervise meals in hospitals, schools and other institutions; supervise the production of food; manage food personnel; manage food purchases.

Aptitudes and Skills: Ability to plan and supervise; to work with people such as other health care professionals. Knowledge of principles of nutrition and foods; of personnel management; of financial management. Interest in science; in serving people. Appreciation for food.

Dispatchers   *Responsibilities:* Relay information, requests and/or written orders; assign personnel and/or vehicles. Maintain radio contact; keep records or requests and services performed; maintain maps showing approximate locations of workers or vehicles.

Aptitudes and Skills: Ability to plan and direct the activities of workers; to speak clearly and distinctly; to react quickly and calmly; to establish priorities rapidly. Good hearing. Good use of fingers and hands.

Drafters

Responsibilities: Translate the ideas and rough sketches of engineers and architects into detailed drawings which enable other workers to manufacture products according to designers' specifications.

Aptitudes and Skills: Ability to visualize objects; to work from written and oral instructions; to do precise and detailed work. Knowledge of the principles and practices of drafting; of tools of the trade.

Ecologists

Responsibilities: Study and solve problems dealing with wildlife control, air, water, land, pollution, resource protection, waste disposal.

Aptitudes and Skills: Ability to analyze, prepare and present scientific information; to work with numbers; to organize information. Knowledge of principles, concepts and methods of environmental control and resource management. Above average intelligence. Curiosity about the interactions in living systems.

Economists

Responsibilities: Study and teach how people use resources such as land, labor, and capital. Analyze the relationship between supply and demand; determine ways in which goods are produced, consumed, and distributed; study problems such as inflation and recession; carry out studies for government to assess economic conditions and the need for changes in economic policy.

Aptitudes and Skills: Knowledge of the principles of economics; of statistics, research methodologies and data analysis. Ability to perform arithmetic operations quickly and accurately; to work with detail; to communicate ideas orally and in writing. Analytical aptitude. Above average intelligence.

Electricians

Responsibilities: Install wiring and maintain electrical equipment such as generators and lighting systems. Inspect and service electronic control devices.

Aptitudes and Skills: Ability to visualize objects of two or three dimensions and make visual comparisons; to apply mathematics to practical problems; to read blueprints; to use and maintain tools and test equipment. Knowledge of electricity; basic electronics; planning and estimating jobs; ordering supplies. Good eye-hand coordination. Good manual dexterity.

Engineers

Responsibilities: Determine how to combine raw materials to produce goods or build projects such as roads, dams, buildings and bridges. Plan and oversee construction and research projects; design, inspect and test equipment, machinery, materials and products. Aerospace engineers design, construct and test aircraft and spacecraft. Civil engineers plan and supervise the construction and maintenance of roads, railroads, airports, bridges, harbors, dams, pipelines, power plants, and water and sewage systems. Electrical engineers design and supervise the manufacturing of electrical and electronic equipment, systems and machinery. Mechanical engineers design tools, engines and machines that produce, transmit and use power.

Aptitudes and Skills: Ability to visualize spatial relations of plane and solid objects; to communicate orally and in writing. Knowledge of engineering and design; of mathematics; of physical and social sciences. High math and science aptitude. Above average intelligence.

Financial Managers

Responsibilities: Analyze facts, prepare financial reports and implement company policies to assure smooth business operations. Work with other company managers to coordinate plans and provide information for policy makers. Manage an organization's finances; manage marketing or research department. Serve as controllers or treasurers.

Aptitudes and Skills: Ability to work with numbers; to work with attention to detail; to negotiate; to analyze and communicate facts; to develop long-range goals and objectives; to plan, direct and coordinate programs; to develop methods of evaluating a company's growth, productivity and ability to reach its goals. Knowledge of principles, methods, techniques and systems of fiscal and business management.

Fish and Wildlife Specialists

Responsibilities: Research and solve problems related to such natural resources as soil, water, plants and animals. Manipulate and manage natural resources for the economic, commercial, recreational and/or aesthetic interest of people. Survey and restore marshes, lakes and streams; manage wildlife refuges and game areas; enforce conservation regulations; educate others about wildlife conservation; work in artificial propagation of fishes and in water quality assessment and control; monitor the timber industry.

Aptitudes and Skills: Knowledge of the specialty area or areas as mentioned above. Ability to work alone as well as with others; to write technical reports; to speak publicly. Self-discipline. High degree of academic ability for those interested in research. Good health.

Foresters

Responsibilities: Strive to achieve the best use of forest land and resources for economic and recreational purpose. Evaluate forest resources; plan and supervise restoration projects; research and develop methods to protect forests from insects and disease; manage wildlife protection and recreation areas.

Aptitudes and Skills: Knowledge of map preparation and reading; of mathematical methods used to estimate future growth; research skills; science; technical report writing; basic administration. Ability to analyze problems related to forest resource management, evaluate alternatives and make recommendations; to work independently. Capacity for details and standards.

Geologists

Responsibilities: Analyze and study the structure, composition and history of the earth. Take samples; apply scientific principles; draw conclusions; prepare reports; make recommendations to oil companies, mining companies, government agencies and universities.

Aptitudes and Skills: Ability to perceive forms and spatial relationships; to communicate orally and in writing; to draw conclusions from limited data. Knowledge of the principles of earth science; of the scientific method; of laboratory and/or field techniques. Inquisitive mind. Extremely high intellectual and mathematical ability.

Graphic Artists

Responsibilities: Create artwork to call attention to products, services or opinions. Produce artwork for publications, billboards, packages in a variety of styles and media. Create original designs and layouts, prepare sketches and draw finished artwork. Choose colors, paste up layouts and mark instructions for printers.

Aptitudes and Skills: Creativity. Ability to visualize two-dimensional representation of objects; to move from abstract ideas to concrete images; to make visual comparisons; to distinguish subtle differences in shapes and colors; to make decisions based on experience.

Health and Safety Inspectors

Responsibilities: Enforce and advise on public health and safety regulations governing work environment, food, drugs and other consumer goods. Work with laboratory scientists and other health workers to find and prevent the spread of disease and to insure the purity of water, air, food and drugs. Visit establishments to investigate sanitary conditions and collect samples. Visit work sites to identify hazards and make sure safety equipment is used. Examine buildings for fire hazards and soundness of construction. Check vehicles for mechanical problems and safety devices. Teach the public about good health and safety practices.

Aptitudes and Skills: Ability to analyze and use facts; to work with little room for error; to interpret and apply federal, state, and local health and safety regulations; to communicate effectively. Knowledge of basic scientific and/or engineering principles and their application to health and safety. Good observation skills.

Hotel/Motel Managers

Responsibilities: Direct the business operations of hotels and motels. Hire personnel; manage purchase of supplies; determine rates and credit policies; direct publicity and advertising efforts. In small firms, perform clerical functions; relieve the desk clerk; relieve the switchboard operator.

Aptitudes and Skills: Ability to work with people and gain their confidence; to communicate verbally and in writing; to perceive clerical detail; to work with numbers. Knowledge of management skills; accounting; purchasing; personnel administration; of hotel operations such as front desk, maintenance, housekeeping, food and drink preparation, service.

Instrument Repairers

Responsibilities: Service, inspect and install delicate instruments and control systems used to measure and regulate machine operations. Repair, adjust or replace units in instruments and systems that measure time, weight, pressure, and fluid flow and record data.

Aptitudes and Skills: Ability to apply prescribed methods and standards; to work independently; to use tools and electronic testing equipment; to read and sketch blueprints; to diagnose and repair problems. Knowledge of electronics; electricity; hydraulics; pneumatics; shop math; instrumentation theory. Mechanical ability. Good eyesight. Good use of hands and fingers.

Insurance Brokers

Responsibilities: Sell policies to individuals and businesses for protection against future losses. Analyze the client's needs and resources; recommend specific amounts and types of insurance; maintain records; prepare reports; identify prospective customers. Assist in collecting premiums and preparing insurance claims for clients.

Aptitudes and Skills: Knowledge of the fundamentals and procedures of insurance selling; of details of specific policy coverage; of laws pertaining to insurance; of laws pertaining to contracts, liabilities, income and inheritance taxes, health plans. Ability to communicate by telephone, in person and in writing. Self-motivation. Self-confidence. Tact. Patience. Persistence. Ability to work under the pressure of sales quotas.

Lawyer *Responsibilities:* Advise clients of their legal rights and obligations and represent them in courts of law. Negotiate out-of-court settlements; represent clients before government agencies; prepare legal documents such as contracts and wills; act as trustees, guardians, or executors.

Aptitudes and Skills: Ability to work with abstract ideas; to deal with complex and detailed work; to reason and analyze; to relate well with people; to speak and write effectively; to conduct research. Knowledge of the law and court procedures. Intelligence. Diligence.

Legal Assistants *Responsibilities:* Assist lawyers. Research and interpret law sources; interview clients for information; prepare legal documents.

Aptitudes and Skills: Ability to work quickly and accurately; to work with a minimum of supervision; to analyze complex and detailed materials; to communicate effectively orally and in writing. Knowledge of legal terminology and procedures; investigation and interview techniques; of particular legal specialties such as corporations, contracts, real estate, domestic relations, estates, trusts and/or probate.

Librarians *Responsibilities:* Organize and coordinate the information contained in libraries. Order, catalogue and classify materials; maintain the library's collection of books, periodicals, and other holdings; prepare reading lists and furnish access to special information as requested.

Aptitudes and Skills: Ability to understand information presented in verbal or tabular manner; to present information and ideas clearly; to plan and carry out programs and procedures; to work well with people of varying abilities and backgrounds. Knowledge of library techniques, systems, and procedures; of the classification and presentation of information in a variety of media.

Loan Officers *Responsibilities:* Evaluate applicants' financial backgrounds to determine whether or not they will receive loans. Review reports of credit analysis; weigh all aspects; make decisions for large institutions.

Aptitudes and Skills: Ability to understand and apply procedures; to make numerical calculations with speed and accuracy. Knowledge of economics. Financial aptitude. Memory for detail.

Market Research Analysts

Responsibilities: Compile industrial or consumer information for use by companies in making decisions on their products and services. Design survey questionnaires, interviews, focus groups, and other techniques to collect data from consumers. Utilize records, trade and other journals, government reports and statistics to gather information. Analyze numerical and verbal data and present written and/or oral reports of conclusions and recommendations.

Aptitudes and Skills: High ability to work well with both words and numbers. Ability to see important detail and patterns in verbal and numerical data. Ability to work well with people. Ability to make decisions based on experience and data.

Mathematicians

Responsibilities: Conduct research and analyze numerical data to provide information to help solve problems in various fields. Organize, analyze, interpret and present information in numerical form. Develop theories, techniques and approaches to solving problems in sciences, engineering and management.

Aptitudes and Skills: Ability to relate and represent abstract ideas by means of symbols; to generalize from the specific; to think abstractly; to present results of statistical analysis both orally and in writing. Knowledge of mathematical and statistical methods and their use in various fields. Numerical, verbal and analytical ability. Interest in research.

Mechanics, Automobile

Responsibilities: Repair and maintain automotive equipment. Carry out preventive maintenance; diagnose failures; replace and repair broken parts.

Aptitudes and Skills: Ability to use tools and equipment of the trade; to make an accurate diagnosis and cost estimate of repair. Knowledge of automobiles and their electrical and mechanical systems. Good use of hands and fingers.

Mechanics, Heating and Cooling

Responsibilities: Install and repair refrigeration and heating equipment in homes, schools, and commercial buildings.

Aptitudes and Skills: Ability to read blueprints and design specifications; to diagnose problems in equipment and make adjustments. Knowledge of sheet metal work; basic electricity; carpentry; electronics; math; welding; soldering; and all equipment of the trade. Mechanical ability. Good eyesight including color vision.

Military, Enlisted Personnel

Responsibilities: Employed in various occupations. See job title closest to military occupation.

Military Officers

Responsibilities: Hold leadership and supervisory positions in all branches of the armed services. Most officers are general administrators with technical and managerial responsibilities.

Aptitudes and Skills: Ability to perform a variety of duties; to lead; to work with people of varied backgrounds. Knowledge of administration and organizations. Must be ready to perform work under combat situations. Self-discipline. Initiative.

Nurses (Licensed Practical Nurses)

Responsibilities: Assist in caring for patients with medical problems. Administer medication; monitor equipment; change dressings; prepare food trays; feed, bathe, massage, and dress patients; maintain patients' charts; take temperatures and pulse rates.

Aptitudes and Skills: Ability to work with people; to administer medication and treat patients according to the doctor's prescription; to observe, report and record patients' conditions. Knowledge of the principles of nursing. Good health. Physical strength. Interest in science.

Nurses (Registered Nurses)   *Responsibilities:* Care for patients and function as a member of the health care team. Provide nursing care for patients; teach health care; instruct other personnel in nursing skills; administer drugs; perform treatments; maintain records.

Aptitudes and Skills: Ability to work with people; to communicate orally and in writing; to prepare and administer treatment and medications; to maintain charts and records accurately. Knowledge of medical terminology; of the principles and practices of nursing. Interest in science.

Office Managers   *Responsibilities:* Organize and evaluate office production and procedures to maintain an efficient flow of work. Supervise office operations; coordinate work schedules; maintain personnel, financial and other office records.

Aptitudes and Skills: Ability to communicate effectively both orally and in writing; to supervise; to evaluate the work of others. Knowledge of standard office practices and office equipment. Good clerical perception.

Opticians   *Responsibilities:* Prepare corrective lenses and eyeglasses according to the prescriptions of ophthalmologists and optometrists. Fit glasses; sell frames; grind, polish and cut lenses; mount lenses in frames.

Aptitudes and Skills: Ability to meet precise standards; to perceive forms and spatial relationships; to meet the public. Knowledge of optical equipment; use of tools; of optical materials; of the anatomy of the eye; of normal and abnormal vision and perception; of federal, state, and local laws governing the opthalmic field.

Optometrists   *Responsibilities:* Help people protect and improve their vision. Examine the eyes to determine the presence of vision impairments, eye diseases, or other malfunctions; prescribe and adapt lenses or other optical aids; utilize vision training to preserve, restore and improve vision.

Aptitudes and Skills: Ability to work with people; to work with small objects. Knowledge of optics; chemistry; pathology; pharmacology; neurology; physiology; anatomy; of special instruments and techniques used to test vision.

Personnel Officers   *Responsibilities:* Plan and implement an organization's policies and programs to attract and maintain the best available personnel. Recruit, interview, and hire job applicants; counsel and discipline employees; classify jobs; prepare wage scales; administer employee benefit and retirement programs; conduct training.

Aptitudes and Skills: Ability to work with people; to communicate both orally and in writing; to keep records; to prepare schedules. Knowledge of interview and evaluation techniques; affirmative action laws; compensation practices.

Pharmacists   *Responsibilities:* Dispense drugs and medicines prescribed by physicians, dentists, and veterinarians. Prepare, compound, package and sell medicines; carry out research in the preparation and effects of new medicines.

Aptitudes and Skills: Ability in science; in math; in clerical perception; ability to deal with the public; to interpret and understand written prescriptions, formulas, and other pharmaceutical information. Knowledge of composition and properties of drugs; of procedures for testing the purity and strength of drugs.

Photographers   *Responsibilities:* Record visual images on film to graphically illustrate or explain an idea. Plan pictures to meet special needs such as those of advertising, journalism, industry, or science; develop the film; prepare the pictures for presentation.

Aptitudes and Skills: Ability to perceive forms and spatial relationships; to perceive colors. Knowledge of camera operations; lighting; composition; darkroom procedures; special properties of films and papers. Good eyesight. Creativity.

Physicians   *Responsibilities:* Maintain and improve the health of their patients. Job duties vary by specialty. There are thirty-four major fields of specialization recognized by the American Medical Association. Diagnose medical problems; prescribe treatments; prevent illness by advising patients on self-care related to diet and exercises; assign routine tasks to other members of the health care team.

Aptitudes and Skills: Ability to make decisions in emergencies; to communicate well both orally and in writing; to work with people. Knowledge of the application of basic science and clinical medicine to the human body; of medical terminology; physical examination procedures; of modern diagnostic procedures and equipment. Above average intelligence required to understand the basic medical sciences. Interest in science. Good judgment. Emotional stability.

Physicists   *Responsibilities:* Seek to find the laws that govern the properties of matter and energy in the universe. Make observations; take measurements; develop new instruments. Conduct basic research to find the answers to fundamental questions; conduct applied research to find the answers to practical problems; work at theoretical levels to develop mathematical models to explain the laws and forces of nature; teach.

Aptitudes and Skills: Ability to visualize objects from drawings and written words; to see detail; to be thorough; to write technical reports. Knowledge of scientific theory; application of scientific theory; of higher math; of laboratory and field techniques; of specialty areas such as solid state, nuclear and astro physics; cryogenics; biophysics; acoustics; atomic and geophysics. High intellectual, numerical and verbal ability. Liking for working with facts.

Pilots and Flight Engineers

Responsibilities: Work as part of a team to operate aircraft. Pilots operate the flight controls; communicate with the crew and with land personnel; monitor flight instruments; supervise the crew. Flight engineers make pre-flight checks; monitor operation of mechanical and electrical systems during flight.

Aptitudes and Skills: Ability to organize and plan; to work under stress; to make quick accurate decisions; to be able to react quickly to different situations. Good emotional and physical health; good hearing; vision not worse than 20/100 correctable to 20/20; excellent eye-hand-foot coordination. Knowledge of instrument reading; weather conditions; algebra; navigation; principles of flight. Leadership.

Production Managers

Responsibilities: Assure the economic and timely production of a firm's products. Analyze data on costs and market conditions; direct activities of subordinate supervisors; interpret statistics on availability of raw materials; supervise maintenance of plant equipment; supervise quality control; keep records of labor, production, material costs and equipment.

Aptitudes and Skills: Ability to coordinate people, materials, time; to plan, initiate and carry out ideas and programs. Knowledge of industry; of equipment; of manufacturing processes; of business and financial management. Facility with numbers and recordkeeping.

Psychologists

Responsibilities: Study the behavior of individuals and groups and try to help people achieve satisfactory personal adjustment. Teach; research; specialize in such areas as learning or perception; provide testing, counseling, treatment in clinics, schools, industries. Perform administrative duties.

Aptitudes and Skills: Ability to communicate well with others; to write well to communicate research and/or diagnostic findings. Knowledge of human motivation; behavior; of diagnostic techniques; of psychotherapeutic techniques; of administration and interpretation of standardized tests; of research procedures. Maturity and emotional stability.

Public Relations Workers

Responsibilities: Aid their clients in building and maintaining favorable public images. Prepare information about their employers for radio, television, newspapers and other media; write speeches; arrange for speaking engagements; participate in community affairs.

Aptitudes and Skills: Ability to write and speak clearly and simply; to work with people; to persuade; to organize and plan; to gather information. Knowledge of clients (individuals or organizations); of journalism; of business administration; of public speaking; of the news media; of public affairs. Originality.

Purchasing Agents

Responsibilities: Buy merchandise, materials, supplies and equipment needed for an organization to function. Analyze needs; develop and write specifications; negotiate with salespeople.

Aptitudes and Skills: Ability to work on details; to work with people; to work easily with numbers; to write clear product specifications. Knowledge of purchasing practices; of contract, property and insurance laws; of sources of supplies; of pricing methods and discounts; of inventory control; of finance; of accounting; statistics; use of computer applications to the field. Knowledge of comparative bidding.

Quality Control Inspectors

Responsibilities: Examine products to assure that set standards are met. Use appropriate measuring instruments; compute mathematics; monitor allowable percentage of defects; recommend changes in production; write final reports.

Aptitudes and Skills: Ability to reason and make judgments; to present information clearly both orally and in writing; to perform numerical operations; to do precise work. Knowledge of the standards to be met in a specific job setting; of appropriate measuring instruments; of laboratory equipment.

Radio and TV Broadcasters

Responsibilities: Provide information and entertainment by talking to audiences over the airwaves. Read news, weather, commercials, sports, station announcements; act; play music; read and log meters (radio only).

Aptitudes and Skills: Ability to meet a tight schedule; to work with people. Knowledge of voice; microphone techniques; studio controls; turntables, tape recorders and other technical equipment; grammar, usage and pronunciation.

Real Estate Appraisers

Responsibilities: Evaluate real estate to determine its value for purchase, tax, investment or loan purposes. May specialize in residential, agricultural or income investment properties. Make inspections; write reports.

Aptitudes and Skills: Ability to catch onto things; to check accuracy; to work with words and numbers; to analyze. Knowledge of the real estate market; of real estate law; of appraising techniques.

Real Estate Brokers

Responsibilities: Bring together buyers and owners of property to work out transactions. Supervise real estate salespeople; sell, exchange, rent real estate for clients; show property; draw up leases, deeds and mortgages.

Aptitudes and Skills: Ability to work with numbers and details; to work with people. Knowledge of sales techniques; financing procedures; business conditions; property values; laws affecting the sale of property; market values; pricing; of clients' needs and resources. Persistence. Tact. Patience. Self-motivation.

Receptionists

Responsibilities: Greet callers at business offices to determine the purpose of their visits and instruct them accordingly. Make appointments; supply requested directions; keep records; send bills; receive payments; type; file; answer telephones.

Aptitudes and Skills: Ability to communicate information accurately; to work with others; to retain a pleasant manner. Knowledge of general office procedures; typing; telephone switchboard operation.

Recreation Program Directors

Responsibilities: Supervise paid and volunteer personnel who plan and run recreational programs in public and voluntary agencies, and private firms. Promote and administer such programs as athletics, outdoor recreation, arts and crafts, recreation for the elderly and the handicapped.

Aptitudes and Skills: Ability to relate to and communicate with others; to plan and implement policies and programs; to establish and maintain good working relationships with staff and clients. Knowledge of a variety of recreational activities; of the personal skill needed to conduct them; of methods of planning, equipping and maintaining recreation facilities; of first aid.

Salesperson

Responsibilities: Provide customers with a general knowledge of products in order to sell the merchandise. Determine the type and quality of merchandise desired; show various items; explain design, quality and usefulness; prepare sales slips; receive payment or credit authorization. Keep sales records; stock shelves; take inventories; set up displays.

Aptitudes and Skills: Ability to communicate clearly; to deal with the public; to stand for long periods of time; to do arithmetic quickly; to analyze the customer's wants. Knowledge of merchandise; sales techniques; forms used.

Sales and Service Managers

Responsibilities: Direct the distribution of products and services to customers in order to increase business. Direct marketing staffs; coordinate the marketing process; establish sales territories, quotas and goals; supervise workers in customer service; monitor recordkeeping; maintain inventories; obtain information from customers on service desired.

Aptitudes and Skills: Ability to plan, initiate and carry out ideas and programs; to supervise staff. Knowledge of product and/or service offered by firm; of sales techniques; of range and scope of services. Leadership. Enthusiasm.

Sales Representatives

Responsibilities: Sell equipment, services, and supplies to wholesale and retail businesses. Travel to customers' businesses; display and demonstrate merchandise; quote prices; prepare sales contracts; solicit business; keep records; participate in collection efforts.

Aptitudes and Skills: Ability to deal effectively with people; to persuade; to work quickly and accurately with numbers; to work under pressure to meet sales quotas; to perceive details; to work without direct supervision. Some jobs require the ability to carry heavy loads; to drive a car. Knowledge of product or services offered for sale; of sales and marketing techniques; of needs of customers; employer's credit, shipping and delivery policies. Initiative. Self-motivation. Patience. Tact.

Secretaries

Responsibilities: Perform a variety of clerical tasks and carry out some executive responsibilities in order to keep the office functioning smoothly. Organize office functions; schedule appointments, screen telephone calls; welcome visitors; type; transcribe; file.

Aptitudes and Skills: Ability to type to minimum of 50 words per minute and/or take shorthand; to follow verbal and written instructions; to operate office machinery; to organize office responsibilities; to spell. Knowledge of wordprocessing helpful; of correct punctuation, a must. Clerical perception.

Social Scientists

Responsibilities: Study human behavior and environment to increase understanding and solve practical problems. Analyze the cultures of various peoples; study the theories and organizations of governments; describe and interpret people and events of the past and present; study the behavior and relationship of groups to individuals and societies; deal with the distribution of people, land and water masses, and natural resources. Work for private and public institutions, government agencies, schools and universities, teaching, carrying out research, and program planning.

Aptitudes and Skills: Knowledge of the principles of sociology, economics, geography or other areas of specialization; of statistics; of research methodologies; of data analysis. High degree of rationality. Clarity of expression. Intellectual capacity to understand the basic principles and methods.

Social Workers

Responsibilities: Help individuals and groups solve their personal and social problems. Interview clients to identify problems; develop plans to meet their needs; determine eligibility for assistance, funds, services; aid clients in securing services; record case programs.

Aptitudes and Skills: Ability to communicate verbally and in writing; to be persuasive; to work with many different kinds of people; to handle large amounts of paperwork. Knowledge of sociology; psychology; economics; current social policies; of counseling and guidance principles and practices; of community resources; of interviewing techniques; of agency policies. Understanding of individual rights and cultural differences. Emotional maturity.

Speech Pathologists

Responsibilities: Help people with speech or hearing problems by examining the disorder and providing treatment. Use oral and written tests to determine speech and language skills; conduct programs to improve communication skills; provide counseling; teach; direct research.

Aptitudes and Skills: Ability to speak and hear well. Knowledge of the processes and disorders of speech, hearing and language; of measurement and evaluation of speech production; of research methodology; of clinical treatment; of training techniques used for individuals with communication disorders. Interest and liking for people. Patience. Emotional stability.

Stockbrokers

Responsibilities: Help people select and purchase stocks, bonds, securities, and mutual funds based on their individual needs. Analyze investments; furnish information about market conditions; distribute information about securities and planning to customers.

Aptitudes and Skills: Ability to deal with people; to work independently; to analyze numbers; to speak effectively.

Knowledge of state and federal laws pertaining to securities; of economic conditions and trends; of security analysis.

Surveyors

Responsibilities: Measure the earth's surface to determine the shape, contour, location and dimension of land and land features. Use information in making maps and charts, establishing construction sites, determining land boundaries. If licensed, may supervise other surveyors.

Aptitudes and Skills: Ability to visualize objects in two or three dimensions; to work with precision instruments; to work outdoors; to sketch plans; to keep notes. Knowledge of math and science; of survey instruments and equipment; of survey and land record laws; of legal principles of land boundaries; of how to write property descriptions; of map-making. Physical stamina.

Systems Analysts

Responsibilities: Plan data processing systems to solve business, scientific, or engineering problems. Examine organizational needs; examine existing data processing systems; confer with managers; perform special studies to test the efficiency of data processing systems. Choose electronic equipment suitable to specific tasks; prepare instructions for programmers. Some complete the programming responsibilities.

Aptitudes and Skills: Ability to organize ideas and data; to analyze and use facts; to communicate effectively orally and in writing. Knowledge of computer concepts and limitations. Numerical ability. Persistence.

Teachers, Elementary and Secondary

Responsibilities: Develop and plan teaching materials. Provide classroom instruction to students. Elementary teachers normally work with one group of pupils during the day. Secondary teachers usually specialize in a subject area and work with four to five groups of students in a day.

Aptitudes and Skills: Ability to relate well with people; to persuade; to organize materials and ideas. Knowledge of the techniques used in communicating and generating knowledge; of how to guide students in the learning process; of the techniques of testing and evaluation. Knowledge of the subject area. Capacity for understanding students. Creativity. Versatility. Patience. Leadership.

Teachers, Performing Arts

Responsibilities: Educate and train students in the fields of acting, dance and music. Prepare courses of study to fit the needs and abilities of students; drill students in techniques; conduct rehearsals; direct performances. May instruct classes or individuals.

Aptitudes and Skills: Ability to communicate; to organize materials and ideas; to present materials on an individual or group basis. Proven proficiency as an actor, actress, singer, musician, dancer. Creativity. Versatility. Patience. Leadership.

Teachers, University and College

Responsibilities: Educate and train students. Prepare and present materials; evaluate students through assigned problems, discussions, research papers, laboratory work and examinations. Engage in research and writing. Serve as advisors to students. Serve as consultants to industry and government.

Aptitudes and Skills: Ability to work with ideas and concepts; to communicate effectively; to relate to a wide variety of students. Knowledge of one's field; of evaluation. Self-discipline. Good judgment.

Technicians, Broadcast

Responsibilities: Install, operate and maintain electronic equipment used to record or transmit radio and television programs.

Aptitudes and Skills: Ability to visualize objects of two or three dimensions; to work under stress. Knowledge of broadcast equipment; of electronics principles; of test equipment such as oscilloscopes; of the use of related tools such as soldering irons. Facility for math. Good color vision.

Technicians, Dental Lab

Responsibilities: Make and repair dentures, crowns, bridges and other dental appliances according to dentists' prescriptions. Study the dentist's prescription; plan the sequence of work; design, construct and repair the dentures.

Aptitudes and Skills: Ability to perceive forms and spatial relationships; to carry out detailed work; to work under pressure to meet deadlines; to use laboratory tools and equipment safely. Knowledge of oral anatomy; dental lab techniques; technical vocabulary; characteristics of materials used. Finger and manual dexterity. Patience. Artistic ability.

Technicians, Electronics

Responsibilities: Help engineers design and develop electronic equipment and electrical machinery. Products include semi-conductors, transformer, computers, industrial and medical measuring or control devices. Use information from blueprints and detailed drawings; test, adjust and inspect products; insure that set standards and specifications have been met; repair and service defective equipment.

Aptitudes and Skills: Ability to express ideas and information clearly both orally and in writing; to work with numbers; to analyze technical information; to notice and compare differences in objects; to work to detailed specifications; to do precise work. Knowledge of math and related fields of science; of technical blueprint reading; drafting; basic electrical engineering procedures.

Technicians, Emergency Medical

Responsibilities: Provide immediate care to the critically ill and injured. May transport patients to hospitals. Determine the nature and extent of illness or injury; provide first aid; lift and carry patients on stretchers; radio the patient's condition to medical personnel at the hospital. Inspect and maintain ambulance and emergency equipment.

Aptitudes and Skills: Ability to work with people who are injured or in a state of shock; able to lift and carry patients. Knowledge of life support and emergency treatment procedures; of the care and use of emergency equipment; of the repair and maintenance of ambulances; of sanitizing and disinfecting procedures.

Technicians, Health

Responsibilities: Use sophisticated medical equipment to aid in the diagnosis and therapy of various health problems. Some technicians specialize in the operation of electrocardiograph, electroencephalograph, or dialysis equipment; others specialize in preparing operating room equipment; others specialize in constructing and fitting braces and artificial limbs.

Aptitudes and Skills: Ability to work with equipment; to work with patients; to perceive forms and spatial relationships. Knowledge of medical equipment; medical terminology.

Technicians, Medical Records

Responsibilities: Maintain files of information on patients for hospitals and other health facilities. Analyze and code information; review records for accuracy; compile statistics; prepare reports; supervise clerks.

Aptitudes and Skills: Ability to work accurately; to communicate orally and in writing; to work with data; to work with people. Knowledge of information storage system; evaluation of health records; medical terminology; statistical recording.

Technicians, Nuclear Power

Responsibilities: Operate machines to produce nuclear fuels and to control nuclear reactors. Control equipment to extract uranium and other radioactive materials; use sandblasting machines and chemicals to clean radioactive equipment; control reactors used in scientific tests; observe gauges; adjust controls; load and unload nuclear fuel elements; seal radioactive waste in lead and concrete containers.

Aptitudes and Skills: Ability to carry out instructions with precision; to deal with stress; to work with machines. Knowledge of nuclear processes and techniques; clerical recordkeeping; mechanics; electronics.

Technicians, Radio and TV Service

Responsibilities: Install and repair electrical and electronic equipment such as radios, tv's, phonographs, tape recorders and electronic instruments.

Aptitudes and Skills: Ability to manipulate parts and tools; to follow diagrams and manufacturers' specifications. Knowledge of basic math; electronics circuitry and components; of appropriate tools and testing devices; of diagnosing problems; of making repairs.

Therapists, Occupational

Responsibilities: Plan and organize activities to help rehabilitate patients who are physically or mentally disabled. Direct educational, vocational and recreational activities; evaluate the abilities and skills of patients; set goals for patients; plan therapy programs; work with other members of the medical staff.

Aptitudes and Skills: Ability to work with others; to communicate with patients and staff; to maintain records of patients' progress. Knowledge of therapy programs; of equipment and materials used in therapy programs; of anatomy; neuroanatomy; kinesiology; activity analysis. Patience. Manual skill. Interest in serving people.

Therapists, Physical

Responsibilities: Treat individuals with physical disabilities to relieve pain and restore function. Plan and administer treatments prescribed by a physician; administer and interpret tests and measurements for muscle strength, coordination, respiratory and circulatory efficiency; develop programs for treatment; instruct patients in the care and use of wheelchairs, braces, crutches and other devices; keep records of treatment.

Aptitudes and Skills: Ability to work toward long-range goals; to work with people; to communicate with patients and members of the medical team. Knowledge of principles, techniques, materials and equipment used in physical therapy; of how to adapt treatment to individual patients; of human growth and development; of human anatomy and physiology; of how to repair and/or construct needed equipment; of community resources. Stamina. Patience. Interest in people.

Travel Agents

Responsibilities: Provide travel information and make travel arrangements which meet client's budget, interest and time. Use timetables, travel manuals, rate books; plan routes; compute costs; verify arrival and departure times and seating space.

Aptitudes and Skills: Ability to work with people; to work with details; to do several things at one time; to work easily on the telephone; to communicate information accurately; to keep up with frequent changes in information.

Underwriters 	*Responsibilities:* Review insurance applications, determine the degree of risk involved, and accept applications following company policy. Look at applications; examine medical reports; review actuarial tables; make judgments; outline the terms of the contract and premium rates. Correspond with policyholders, agents, and managers. Specialize in life, property and liability, or health insurance policies for individuals or groups.

Aptitudes and Skills: Ability to make prompt decisions; to communicate with others; to catch onto things easily; to work with details; to gather and evaluate information; to write reports. Knowledge of company's policies; of the various types of insurance; of methods of rating policies; of statistical interpretation.

Urban and Regional Planners 	*Responsibilities:* Prepare for the overall growth and improvement of urban, suburban, and rural areas. Plan for solutions to problems in areas such as land use, housing, transportation and environmental resources. Prepare studies that show how land is currently being used; propose ways to develop unused land; suggest improvements to existing facilities to meet future needs. Meet with citizens' groups. Speak before planning committees.

Aptitudes and Skills: Ability to work with people; to communicate orally and in writing; to make evaluations; to work with data; to visualize objects mentally; to perceive detail. Knowledge of governmental organizations and regulations; of the principles of planning; of social and environmental problems.

Veterinarians

Responsibilities: Prevent, control and cure animal diseases. Diagnose and prescribe treatment for companion animals and herd animals. Carry out regulatory and public health functions; research; teach; supervise veterinary technicians.

Aptitudes and Skills: Ability to work with animals. Knowledge of animal anatomy; physiology; pathology; biochemistry; diagnosis and treatment of animal disease; surgical techniques. Intelligence. Manual dexterity. Interest in science.

Word Processing Machine Operators

Responsibilities: Type and edit documents on electronic typewriting equipment. Receive material to type in either handwritten or typed form or on prerecorded cassettes; format the document; type the text; submit the text for proofreading; use the text editing functions of the machine to correct copy.

Aptitudes and Skills: Ability to understand and carry out instructions; to check accuracy; to distinguish between different types of documents; to type a minimum of 50 to 60 words per minute. Knowledge of formats for letters, statistical reports, and other documents; of automatic typewriters, keyboards with video screens, microcomputers as they relate to word processing; of spelling, grammar, and punctuation.

Writers and Editors

Responsibilities: Communicate news and ideas as accurately and clearly as possible to specific audiences. Gather and evaluate facts; write stories or articles; produce technical reports; write advertising copy. Edit material so that it fits the style and space for which it is intended.

Aptitudes and Skills: Ability to understand and use words effectively; to work under pressure; to type; to spell correctly; to understand the nuances of English grammar; to collect data; to verify facts; to analyze. Knowledge of significant issues and interests of readers; of the fundamentals of writing; of the principles of proofreading and preparing copy for printing. For those working with newspapers, ability to use video display terminals.

Writers, Freelance

Responsibilities: Inform and entertain their readers in all forms of creative literary composition. Freelance writers are self-employed although they frequently contract with publishers for specific assignments.

Aptitudes and Skills: Ability to understand and use words effectively; to adapt writing style and content for specific publication; to identify with others and their experiences; to research; to meet deadlines; to write. Creativity. Self-discipline.

VGM CAREER BOOKS

CAREER DIRECTORIES
Careers Encyclopedia
Dictionary of Occupational
    Titles
Occupational Outlook
    Handbook

CAREERS FOR
Animal Lovers
Bookworms
Computer Buffs
Crafty People
Culture Lovers
Environmental Types
Film Buffs
Foreign Language Aficionados
Good Samaritans
Gourmets
History Buffs
Kids at Heart
Nature Lovers
Night Owls
Number Crunchers
Plant Lovers
Shutterbugs
Sports Nuts
Travel Buffs

CAREERS IN
Accounting; Advertising;
Business; Child Care;
Communications; Computers;
Education; Engineering;
the Environment; Finance;
Government; Health Care;
High Tech; Journalism; Law;
Marketing; Medicine;
Science; Social &
Rehabilitation Services

CAREER PLANNING
Admissions Guide to Selective
    Business Schools
Beating Job Burnout
Beginning Entrepreneur
Career Planning &
    Development for College
    Students & Recent Graduates
Career Change

Careers Checklists
Cover Letters They Don't
    Forget
Executive Job Search Strategies
Guide to Basic Cover Letter
    Writing
Guide to Basic Resume Writing
Guide to Temporary
    Employment
Job Interviews Made Easy
Joyce Lain Kennedy's Career
    Book
Out of Uniform
Resumes Made Easy
Slam Dunk Resumes
Successful Interviewing for
    College Seniors
Time for a Change

CAREER PORTRAITS
Animals   Nursing
Cars   Sports
Computers   Teaching
Music   Travel

GREAT JOBS FOR
Communications Majors
English Majors
Foreign Language Majors
History Majors
Psychology Majors

HOW TO
Approach an Advertising
    Agency and Walk Away with
    the Job You Want
Bounce Back Quickly After
    Losing Your Job
Choose the Right Career
Find Your New Career Upon
    Retirement
Get & Keep Your First Job
Get Hired Today
Get into the Right Business
    School
Get into the Right Law School
Get People to Do Things Your
    Way
Have a Winning Job Interview

Hit the Ground Running in
    Your New Job
Improve Your Study Skills
Jump Start a Stalled Career
Land a Better Job
Launch Your Career in TV
    News
Make the Right Career Moves
Market Your College Degree
Move from College into a
    Secure Job
Negotiate the Raise You
    Deserve
Prepare a Curriculum Vitae
Prepare for College
Run Your Own Home Business
Succeed in College
Succeed in High School
Write a Winning Resume
Write Successful Cover Letters
Write Term Papers & Reports
Write Your College Application
    Essay

OPPORTUNITIES IN
This extensive series provides
detailed information on nearly
150 individual career fields.

RESUMES FOR
Advertising Careers
Banking and Financial Careers
Business Management Careers
College Students &
    Recent Graduates
Communications Careers
Education Careers
Engineering Careers
Environmental Careers
50 + Job Hunters
Health and Medical Careers
High School Graduates
High Tech Careers
Law Careers
Midcareer Job Changes
Sales and Marketing Careers
Scientific and Technical Careers
Social Service Careers
The First-Time Job Hunter

VGM Career Horizons
a division of *NTC Publishing Group*
4255 West Touhy Avenue
Lincolnwood, Illinois 60646-1975

GAVILAN COLLEGE LIBRARY

Reference
1 week circulation
no renewals

Date Due

NOV 07 1996	APR 0 7 2000			
MAY 2 1 1997	NOV 1 3 2001			
JUL 1 4 1997				
FEB 1 2 1998				
SEP 1 1 1998				
NOV 3 0 1998				
NOV 2 3 1999				

BRODART, INC.   Cat. No. 23 231   Printed in U.S.A